Success With Science: The Winners' Guide to High School Research

Five Harvard students and research competition winners reveal how to succeed at high school research.

Shiv Gaglani
with
Maria Elena De Obaldia
Scott Duke Kominers
Dayan Li
Carol Y. Suh

Foreword by Nobel Laureate Dudley R. Herschbach
www.successwithscience.org

Published by Research Corporation for Science Advancement

Design by Godat Design

ISBN 0-9633504-8-X

RESEARCH CORPORATION
for **SCIENCE ADVANCEMENT**
A foundation dedicated to science since 1912.

4703 East Camp Lowell Drive, Suite 201
Tucson Arizona 85712

Contents

Dedicated to our parents, teachers, and mentors for
their invaluable encouragement, guidance, and support.

Note from the Publisher

This is an important book, and here is why:

For roughly 60 years the United States has been the world leader in science, technology and engineering. As a result, Americans have enjoyed the benefits of great prosperity, comparatively speaking, undergirded by the national security provided by the world's most advanced and formidable military. It has been a great run.

But now other nations, which have been paying close attention to our successes over the past six decades, are coming on strong. They, too, realize the necessity for excellence in science, technology and engineering. They are working diligently to improve basic and advanced science education in their schools and universities; and, as a result, their economies and their military prowess will increase dramatically in coming decades. There is a very real possibility that within the lifetimes of today's high school students, the U.S. will no longer be the world's preeminent scientific and technological leader.

In a way, this is a good thing. It would mean that perhaps billions of people have been lifted from poverty to prosperity; that millions of additional minds are well educated and performing at peak capacity for—one can only hope—the overall betterment of humankind.

Even if such a bright future comes to pass, however, it is unlikely that economic competition will fade, or that security issues will somehow magically disappear. In fact, given the long view of human history from which we judge these things, one can reasonably assume there will continue to be tensions, insecurities and economic challenges. In such a world, the real world of the 21st century, the United States must provide for its citizens the very best science education the world has to offer, if only to remain among the top tier of prosperous and secure nations.

The book you are now reading is quite likely a key to that future.

It directly addresses America's top high school science students—the very citizens who must one day, and sooner rather than later, face the grand challenges looming before us. These students, more than any other natural resource I can think of, constitute our true national treasure. These are the people who will guide American problem-solving more than half way through the current century.

Fortunately, today's top American science students are equal to the cream of the crop anywhere in the world. This despite a broadly spotty and troubled education "system" that, overall, suffers from poor funding, garbled curricula and a profound dearth of qualified primary and secondary science teachers. Furthermore, at the university level, especially at many large research universities, there persists a "sink-or-swim" arrogance among science departments when it comes to dealing with undergraduates. This attitude is not much of a problem for the very brightest students, but it constitutes a disservice to all the others, from whose ranks might otherwise one day come astonishing insights, or the next "insanely great" idea, were it not for the tragedy of someone setting aside dreams of a science career because his or her university is more focused on research and obtaining federal grant money to support it than on creating highly effective undergraduate science courses.

We are just lucky this is a very big nation, with pockets of excellence at all levels scattered here and there as if by the wind; and it is from these pockets of excellence that our best and brightest emerge to take part in the intensive national science competitions detailed in this book. The importance of these competitions cannot be underestimated. As you peruse these chapters, composed by some very wise Harvard students specifically for their younger siblings in science (in the best tradition of students working collaboratively to help their fellow students), note a couple of broad themes among the reams of very specific and useful words of practical advice.

Note, please, the various discussions and comments about the strong sense of community these competitions engender in their participants. One reason Research Corporation for Science Advancement agreed to fund this book is that we strongly believe in creating communities of knowledge across the various scientific disciplines to tackle the big, increasingly complex problems our world is facing. Long gone are the days when a lone scientist working in ivory tower isolation could solve some deeply puzzling aspect of the natural world, or, while going it alone, come up with the breakthrough solution to a pressing major problem. Science, after two centuries of breathtaking discovery and achievement, has become the victim of its own success, in that the problems are much harder, and the scales at which cutting-edge research occurs are, large or small, vastly beyond our everyday human scale.

Note also the repeated reassurances to high school readers that it is OK if one doesn't take first place in a major science competition, and that it is the process of participation itself that is uniquely valuable. This message comes close to what RCSA has been telling early career scientists, and anyone who will listen, really: Researchers must take more risks to achieve breakthrough discoveries; and even a "failed" experiment, if well thought out, will yield useful knowledge.

The world today's high school science students are inheriting urgently demands that they come up with breakthrough discoveries—the global population is going from more than 6.5 billion today to about ten billion in a mere 40 years. The best minds on our planet have worried aloud and repeatedly that our current infrastructure cannot support such a huge increase without chaos and strife. Never has the need for boldly innovative researchers and top-flight science educators been greater than it is right now.

By 2012 Research Corporation for Science Advancement will have been supporting and encouraging bright young minds to do great things for 100 years. The Foundation was instrumental in supporting Robert Goddard's early work in liquid-fueled rocketry; it helped Ernest Lawrence build the first big cyclotron for atomic research; it underwrote the efforts of a lone wolf researcher named Grote Reber to develop the field of radio astronomy; over the years it has supported the early career research of 40 scientists who went on to win Nobel prizes. We continue that work today through our various programs supporting early career scientist-educators.

By supporting this useful book, RCSA hopes to begin a long and productive collaboration with the rising generation of America's finest minds, and our greatest hope for a better tomorrow.

James M. Gentile
President and CEO
Research Corporation for Science Advancement

Foreword

This is an admirable and unique book. It is a gem among several ambitious projects undertaken by the Harvard College Undergraduate Research Association. The HCURA was founded in 2007 by a group of students, largely freshmen and sophomores. Led by Shiv Gaglani ('10) as president, the basic aim was to foster and broaden opportunities for undergrads to pursue research "early and often." I gladly agreed to be a faculty advisor, much impressed with the evangelical fervor of HCURA members. Soon HCURA launched workshops designed to improve presentation and writing skills, journal clubs to discuss exemplary papers, and faculty seminars and lab tours to acquaint members with research prospects. The Association also inaugurated annual symposia presenting undergraduate research. In April 2009 HCURA extended its research symposium to bring together students from eight colleges in the first such Boston-area meeting.

Meanwhile, Shiv had recruited a team of colleagues that began work on this *Guide*, designed to help high school students develop suitable projects for top-notch science fairs. This was entirely on their own initiative, motivated by appreciation for how much they had benefited from their precollege experience in such fairs. Shiv's team took a novel approach by sending out an email questionnaire to a host of students and faculty mentors (many not at Harvard). Thereby the *Guide*, as well as offering much useful information and advice, has been enhanced by many personal commentaries that provide insightful perspectives on all aspects of science fairs and kindred activities.

Also cited abundantly in the *Guide* are lively interviews of students on site at science fairs, filmed by Dr. Jeffrey Seeman of the University of Richmond. These are available on a website (*Archimedesinitiative.org*) as a set of 17 five-minute videos, each comprised of responses addressing a specific theme. Among the themes are: Decoding the Data; (Self) Discovery Channel; Eureka! Cornering Conclusions; Holding Court with Judges; Conquering Fear, Building Confidence. Like the commentaries in the *Guide*, these interviews bring forth the earnest joy that students get in probing a question of their own choice. And then being rewarded, often after overcoming puzzlement by much effort, with genuine insight and the pleasure of sharing it with others.

I have shown the *Guide* manuscript to numerous faculty colleagues as well as to people long involved in conducting science fairs. All find it remarkably well done and are impressed that Shiv and his team produced this book while also engaged in much else, not least their demanding academic programs. Several faculty asked for copies to give to their graduate students, saying that the *Guide* can surely boost their research by virtue of both its practical advice and its zestful spirit.

The *Guide* is also heartening in the wider context of improving science education, today a vital national goal. The importance of informal modes, allied to but outside schools, is increasingly recognized. It is a privilege to applaud the *Guide*, the enterprise of its youthful authors, and the support given with alacrity by Research Corporation for Science Advancement.

Dudley Herschbach
Frank B. Baird, Jr. Professor of Science, Emeritus, Harvard University
Cambridge, Massachusetts

Preface

Welcome to *The Winners' Guide to High School Research*! First, congratulations are in order because you have already taken the first steps towards succeeding with science by picking up this book. There are many ways to succeed in high school, though there are few that can parallel science research in terms of the widespread opportunities and immense benefits it provides to students who excel in it—hence the title *Success with Science*. The tagline is *The Winners' Guide to High School Research* because this is a guide written by, and containing the advice of, students who have performed extremely well in science research competitions such as the Intel International Science and Engineering Fair, Siemens Competition, and Intel Science Talent Search, among many others.

By reading this book and using the advice within it, you will learn how to formulate a research project idea, find people who can help you complete it, effectively present it to diverse audiences, and participate successfully in research competitions. This guide was written for any high school student interested in science research: from the freshman rookie with a vague interest in science to the senior veteran striving for first place at the Intel Science Talent Search. With its testimonials from high school students whose lives were positively changed by their research experiences, this guide also aims to motivate and empower students who otherwise would not pursue science and research opportunities. In doing so, this book seeks to encourage more students to pursue science and technology, or at least to think creatively and take initiative.

With these ambitious goals in mind, what is the best way to use this book? When I developed the idea and outline of this guide, I chose to divide it into five distinct parts that may be read sequentially or separately depending upon your interests and needs. I recruited four of my peers to be contributing authors based on their experiences and strengths, which are reflected in each part. Part I details the many individual benefits you can realize from participating in science research. For example, many high school students who do research get into top colleges, win scholarships, learn about career options, make lifelong friends, and develop qualities and skills that will help them throughout their life—the chapters in Part I describe each of these benefits in depth.

After Part I whets your appetite to do research, Part II describes the nuts and bolts of getting started by forming an idea, finding a lab or mentor, working in the lab, impressing your mentor, and keeping records of your research in a logbook. Once you make some progress on your project, Part III will help you present your research—in both written reports and oral presentations—to your teachers, science competition judges, and the general public. Part IV not only describes the major research competitions in which you can enter your project and the summer research programs in which you can participate, but also provides advice from actual winners and participants on how to do your best in those venues. Finally, Part V provides a glimpse of what research is like after high school, because there are key differences in college, and knowledge of these differences will help you hit the ground running when you are an undergraduate.

One important note that cannot be overemphasized is that your science research experience will prime you for success, especially if you approach it with a genuine interest in research and discovery rather than an interest in winning competitions. Though the awards and prestige that come with winning are great byproducts of excellent research, the research experience itself is far more valuable in the long-term. Best of luck with your research career!

Shiv Gaglani
Primary Author and Editor
Success with Science: The Winners' Guide to High School Research
Cambridge, Massachusetts

Acknowledgments

There are many people who helped make this book possible. First, we would like to thank Professor Dudley R. Herschbach for his tremendous support and encouragement. He is the co-advisor of the Harvard College Undergraduate Research Association (HCURA), of which we all have been members. We would like to thank HCURA—especially Lev Shaket, Koning Shen, Wendy Ying, Alex Bick, and HCURA co-advisor Greg Llacer—for empowering us to reach out to countless students, teachers, and professionals regarding this project. In the same vein, we would like to thank those students, teachers, and professionals who contributed invaluable advice and quotes to this book.

In terms of the publishing process, we are indebted to Malorie Snider for her help contacting publishers and proofreading the manuscript, Poonam Sharma for her early advice on publishing a book while in college, and William Kominers, Ellen Dickstein Kominers, Saritha K. Tice, Sidney Dickstein, and Jon Grossman for their advice. Last but not least, we are very thankful to Research Corporation for Science Advancement for publishing this manuscript and, in particular, Dan Huff whose energy, helpfulness, and patience throughout the process helped turn this project into a reality.

Shiv Gaglani

Shiv is grateful to all of his high school research teachers at West Shore High and supporters in Brevard County, especially Sherie Jenkins, Tonya Galaida, and Richard DiPatri, as well as his mentors at the University of Central Florida, University of Miami, Clemson University, and Harvard University. He is especially thankful to his RSI mentor, Dr. Glenn D. Rosen, for his guidance over the last five years, as well as to Dr. Nelson Ying for his tremendous support throughout high school and into college. He would also like to thank Professor Dudley R. Herschbach, whom he met at the International Science and Engineering Fair years before entering Harvard. Little did he know that Professor Herschbach would be his advisor, mentor, supporter, and friend throughout his college years. Finally, he is grateful to his sister, Anushka, for always believing in him, and his parents, Dr. Mukesh Gaglani and Vanita Gaglani, for the sacrifices they made so that he could begin this journey, for the continuous support that has allowed him to come this far, and for the lessons in character that give him strength and guidance each day.

Maria Elena De Obaldia

Ellen is grateful for the mentorship of her professors at the University of Pennsylvania and the Children's Hospital of Boston for instilling her with a deep appreciation for science. Ellen is thankful for scholarship and grant support from the United States Navy, Army, Intel Corporation,

Siemens Foundation, the Harvard College Financial Aid program, and the National Institutes of Health. Ellen is deeply grateful to her parents for encouraging her to take on big challenges and seeing her through the obstacles that have come along with this. She is also grateful for her family and friends, who have supported her thus far in countless ways.

Scott Duke Kominers

Scott appreciates the support of his undergraduate research advisors (Susan Athey, Erik D. Demaine, Drew Fudenberg, Edward L. Glaeser, John William Hatfield, William R. Kerr, Alvin E. Roth, Kay Kaufman Shelemay, Andrei Shleifer, David Smith, E. Glen Weyl, and especially Noam D. Elkies), his Research Science Institute mentors (Christopher C. Mihelich, John Rickert, Jenny Sendova, and Aaron M. Tievsky), and his high school teachers (especially Susan Schwartz Wildstrom). While writing his *Guide* chapters, Scott was supported by a Harvard College PRISE Fellowship and a Harvard Mathematics Department Highbridge Fellowship, and by the Harvard IQSS Summer Research Scholars Program. During revision of the manuscript, Scott was supported by an NSF Graduate Research Fellowship. Many of Scott's friends provided helpful comments and suggestions on this work: most notably, Zachary Abel, Andrea J. Hawksley, Sonia Jaffe, Greg Llacer, and Steffano U. Saldrium. Additionally, Scott would like to thank his family for their energy and inspiration.

Dayan (Jack) Li

Dayan is greatly indebted to his high school science and math mentors Jane Hemelt, Rocco Mennella, Godfrey Rangasammy, and all of his teachers at Eleanor Roosevelt High School for inspiring and guiding him through his first forays into scientific research; he also gives special thanks to Dr. David Roberts and Dr. Jeffrey Isenberg for introducing him to the challenges and promises biomedical research at the National Institutes of Health. At Harvard, he has continuously received encouragement and support from faculty, mentors, fellow students, and the administration. Jack thanks Professor Andrew P. McMahon for serving as his lab supervisor, mentor, teacher, and a friend always full of wisdom and advice. He is also deeply grateful to Professor Benjamin Allen, Dr. Zhijun Chen, Dr. Bodo Stern, and Professor Dudley Herschbach for nourishing his growth as a young scientist. Finally and most dearly, he thanks his parents, Chaoxia He and Wenbin Li, and his brother John Li for making everything he does possible and for always believing in him.

Carol Y. Suh

Carol is especially thankful to her high school science fair adviser, Peter Starodub, for his continuous support; her high school research advisers: Dr. Hsian-Rong Tseng, Dr. Kenichiro Kamei, Dr. Guodong Sui, Dr. Harold Martinson, the Martinson lab; and her undergraduate research advisers Dr. David Scadden, Dr. Andre Catic, Dr. Laurence Daheron, Gregory Llacer, and Dr. Debra Peattie for all of their invaluable mentorship and guidance in her development as a scientist. Carol would also like to thank all her teachers, mentors, friends, and family for their guidance, encouragement, and support throughout high school and beyond.

Part I:
The Benefits of Doing Research

1

Why Do Research?

Doing research in high school changed my life. I gained a love for scientific research that my classes never had a chance at conveying, and I learned a lot about myself and what I could do. The research I did in high school [helped to gain] me acceptance at the top colleges I was interested in, [and] the scholarships I won gave me the chance to feasibly attend MIT. My science fair projects were what really allowed me to develop my interest in astronomy, physics, chemistry and spectroscopy.
Mary Masterman: *First Place, Intel Science Talent Search; First Place in Physics, Intel International Science and Engineering Fair; Research Science Institute; MIT Class of 2011*

In this chapter, we will elaborate on the reasons why so many students are starting to do research so early.

Scientists no longer fit the stereotype of old, beaker-carrying men who have regrettably bad hair days. Successful female and male scientists now range from ten to 90 years old. Research has become increasingly accessible in the last few decades, with more secondary school students than ever before conducting scientific experiments. Not only are the researchers becoming younger, the projects are becoming progressively more sophisticated.

Two major factors are responsible for this trend: increased resources and greater encouragement. Students in the 21st century have unprecedented access to a wealth of information via the Internet. High school students are no longer confined to looking up "Pouiselle's Law" in an encyclopedia if they are interested in factors determining blood flow; many now have online access to academic journals such as *Nature* and *Science* that detail the current research on factors affecting blood flow. Knowledge has the habit of breeding even more questions and topics for research. We are reminded of KC Freeman's saying, "The more I learn, the more I realize what little I know." Secondly, there are hundreds of initiatives that aim to inspire young students to pursue careers in science and engineering. Since scientific and technological innovations drive progress, it is important to foster the research growth of students at an early age. Many institutions offer scholarships, competitions and summer programs to achieve this goal. This combination of increased resources and encouragement is a winning formula for inspiring students to do research.

Some students may not be content with just memorizing and regurgitating scientific facts. Others may never blindly agree with what they learn in the classroom. What do these students have in common? A pleasure in discovering something for themselves. Being able to contribute to the pool of human knowledge is often more rewarding than other high school activities, such as getting straight A's or earning a Varsity letter (though by no means are these mutually exclusive!) The motivation to do research has to be much stronger than that, however, if we are to account for the tens of thousands of high school students who do research each year.

By no means is research easy; it can be a substantial time commitment and quite frustrating at times. At the same time, though, it can be the most fulfilling activity of your high school career. The stoichiometric relationship between research and class work is close to 1:3. That is, in one month of research a student can often learn as much as he or she would in three months of schoolwork. Unlike homework, research does not just provide book knowledge. It also enables one to develop important life skills such as giving presentations, writing research papers and applications, networking and making professional boards or posters. This *Guide* aims to set you up for a productive and enjoyable research experience so you can maximize these benefits.

Table 1 summarizes the benefits and costs of doing research in high school and clearly shows there is more to gain from research than there is to lose.

Table 1

Costs vs. Benefits of Research in High School

Benefits	Costs
Personal development	Time consuming
Scholarships	Frustrating at times
College admissions	Hard work
Career decisions	
Expense-paid trips	

In the next few chapters of Part I, we will elaborate on each of these benefits of research in high school.

Take-Home Points

- Tens of thousands of high school students do research each year.
- The benefits of high school research include developing on a personal level, winning scholarships and expense-paid trips, gaining admission to top colleges and learning about career options.
- Visit the Archimedes Initiative *(www.archimedesinitiative.org)* to see the topical videos, "Why You Should Do a Science Fair Project," "What I Enjoyed," and "Making a Difference."

In Their Words

"The research that I did in high school really cemented my love of science. Growing up, I always felt somewhat detached from textbook chapters and lectures. So actually practicing the process of science and discovery through research was important for me. I grew as a person for sure. The work that I was doing was an outlet for my creativity and a chance to express myself much like an artist. The fact that I did my high school research in public health and epidemiology broadened my definition of scientific research—not all of it is done at a lab bench. To have that specific realization as a high school student was eye-opening. I'll be completing a bachelors degree in chemistry and chemical biology this year at Cornell University, so I guess you could say that winning a science competition not only helped me get into a top college (and pay for it!) but also guided my decision to pursue a career in research."
Aman Prasad: *First Place, Young Epidemiology Scholars Competition; Cornell Class of 2010*

"I learned a lot while doing my research: how to plan, how to fix mistakes, what hard work feels like. I did get accepted into a top college (I'm attending MIT), and I won scholarships, but most importantly, I found something I enjoyed. I don't know if I would be an engineer today if I had not done research in high school. I've learned to look at the world around me and try to figure out how everyday things work and why they behave the way they do."
Amber Hess: *First Place in Chemistry, Intel International Science and Engineering Fair; Finalist, Intel Science Talent Search; Semifinalist, Siemens Competition; MIT Class of 2009*

"More than anything I've learned through classes, real hardcore research lifted me from the constrained perspective of a biology student and offered me an overwhelming and inspiring panorama of the dynamic, interactive knowns and unknowns about how our bodies work. Having participated in and presented my research in high school, I feel empowered and entitled to explore a piece of this vast terrain of knowledge. Also, high school research gave me an idea of how scientists think, work and communicate. To me, the most important benefit of high school research has been opening my eyes to the exciting—the world-changing—possibilities of rigorous science."
Dayan Li: *Intel Foundation Young Scientist, Intel International Science and Engineering Fair; Semifinalist, Intel Science Talent Search; Harvard Class of 2011*

"Performing research throughout high school, in conjunction with participating in competitions, has helped me to grow as an individual and scholar. I have formed invaluable relationships that will last the rest of my life."
Lauren R. Lisann: *Finalist, Intel Science Talent Search; Semifinalist, Siemens Competition; Winner, American Academy of Neurology Neuroscience Research Prize; Yale Class of 2012*

"Research is an extremely rewarding and exciting academic experience. There are numerous benefits that come with it. Through research and science fair competitions, I have gained more confidence, willpower and a love for science. The weeks I spent at ISEF in the past two years have been amazing, fulfilling and humbling life experiences. Besides growing as a person, research also helped me win scholarships and get accepted into colleges. I also became more and more interested in pursuing a career in science."
Xiaoli Mi: *Finalist, Intel International Science and Engineering Fair; Harvard Class of 2012*

"When you're going out there to look for research opportunities, just make sure you're having fun with it. More than anything else—more than getting positive results, more than scholarships, more than for college acceptances—make sure that you enjoy what you're doing. Throughout high school I found science research to be one of the most enjoyable things I ever did, in and out of class. Sure, there were times when it seemed like a lot of work and a project sort of consumed my life, but I learned a great deal and grew considerably from my experiences at different presentations. When I hit upon a topic that interested me, it didn't require as much external motivation to keep going, and my curiosity was what pulled me along."
Nolan Kamitaki: *Davidson Fellow; Second Place in Medicine and Health, Intel International Science and Engineering Fair; Semifinalist, Intel Science Talent Search; Semifinalist, Young Epidemiology Scholars Competition; Finalist, Junior Science and Humanities Symposium; Waiakea High School Class of 2010*

"One major benefit of doing research in high school has been learning scientific concepts to a much deeper and broader extent than I ever could just sitting in a classroom or reading a textbook. Research has also helped me think imaginatively; I've learned to follow my hunches, conduct experiments and analyze data rigorously and in new ways, and solve problems unconventionally. It's also made me more resilient to frustration (which I've learned is common in research) as I've continued searching and trying new ideas even when facing what looked like dead ends. The exhilaration of finally hitting on a solution more than makes up for the dispiriting weeks and sometimes months of no apparent progress.

Through research I've also become comfortable taking risks and making mistakes, ingredients I believe to be the key to creativity and discovery. Instead of waiting for my mentor to tell me what to do next, I've come up with my own ideas, sometimes wild ones, and I find that trying them out is highly instructive and productive, even when my experiment has failed. But I've also learned the discipline of thinking deeply about a problem or idea and then carefully and accurately planning, carrying out, and recording my work. Research has also sparked my interest in a cross-disciplinary research and teaching career, because I find the excitement of scientific discovery coupled with the opportunity of explaining and discussing scientific concepts across all scientific disciplines enormously fun.

Another important benefit of doing research has been learning to write scientifically as I've co-authored scientific papers and grant proposals. My research continues to lead to more exciting opportunities, such as co-founding and co-owning a start-up company called Graphene Solutions, which just won the Wisconsin Governor's Business Plan award and has, in turn, attracted venture capital. I've also gained experience with patents as I've worked with patent attorneys on writing and submitting multiple patent disclosures and licenses to the University of Wisconsin.

Research has also given me a new and exciting social world through my involvement in science competitions, where I've met and made friends with fascinating people from around the globe who share my passion for science. This is something I would otherwise never have had the chance to do as a homeschooler living on a farm in rural Southwest Wisconsin. Winning by the end of my junior year in high school over $100,000 in cash and scholarships as well as a free trip to China has been another huge benefit. These competitions have also given me invaluable experience and confidence presenting and defending my ideas before all kinds of audiences. Also, it's been fun to explain and discuss my work with experts

in the field and work alongside and share ideas with other researchers in the lab, many of whom have become my good friends."
Philip V. Streich: *Intel Foundation Young Scientist, Intel International Science and Engineering Fair; Third Place, Intel Science Talent Search; Regional Finalist, Siemens Competition; Davidson Fellow Laureate; United States Physics Olympiad Team; Harvard Class of 2013*

"Deep within the heart of American students is the breaking of traditional rote learning. The rich education experience of science research entices these young students into a new and exciting world of inquiry-based learning. Traditional science education relies on memorization of an incredible amount to information; research experiences make that information come alive to the student."
Joan M. Messer: *Co-Director, American Junior Academy of Science*

Chapter 1

2

Personal Development

Success is not a place at which one arrives but rather the spirit with which one undertakes and continues the journey.
Alex Noble

How can you know what you are truly capable of if you never really challenge yourself? Conducting research is not only a great way to develop your academic abilities and interests, but also to grow as a person and develop interpersonal skills that will serve you for the rest of your life. High school student Natalie Saranga Omattage says that in addition to allowing her to explore many fields of study within the scientific world, "research had a direct influence on my character. I grew to be independent, intelligible, gained more confidence and my public speaking skills improved greatly." Ms. Omattage developed a biosensor to detect hazardous contaminants in food, earning her the prestigious Intel Young Scientist Award at the Intel International Science and Engineering Fair (ISEF). Many students across the country have had similar positive experiences which have shaped their personal lives and careers, though no two students will experience exactly the same journey.

As is the case for most opportunities, the benefits you will take from your research experience will depend on the level of effort you put into it. Participating in research requires that you be willing to invest a significant amount of your time and effort for an uncertain return. There are no guarantees that your experiment will work or that you will be recognized in science competitions for your efforts; however, simply by opening yourself up to the risk of failure, you distinguish yourself from many of your peers. In the process of conducting research, you will learn self-reliance and how to call upon your own unique talents to accomplish your goals. Rather than being discouraged by all the obstacles in your way and giving up before you ever begin, you will learn to focus on what you *can* do. If you make a genuine effort to research something that truly fascinates you, you will be certainly rewarded with knowledge and the satisfaction of a job well done. It is likely that recognition will follow, too. If you are dedicated, your personal development in this process is inevitable.

High school research is ideal for students who want to dig deeper into the material they have learned in school. Research is also a great way to explore entirely new areas of science, engineering and mathematics that are not covered in high school curricula. With support from mentors, almost any field of inquiry is open to you. One of the great things about doing independent research is that you can choose the topic. Conducting research is a great way to become an "expert" on a field or topic that excites you. You need not have taken a course on a subject in order to conduct research on it. Be bold, step outside your comfort zone, challenge yourself every step of the way. Gaining deep knowledge of a specific topic and being able to share that knowledge with others is satisfying and empowering. Once you have the experience of carrying a research project through from start to finish, you will gain confidence that equips you to take on new, diverse challenges in the future. The self-assurance you develop in the research arena will spill over into many different areas of your life. Furthermore, most students we surveyed agree it is possible for this experience to forever expand your horizons and change what you believe is possible for you to achieve. Jue Judy Liu credits her high school research experiences for directing her toward a research career: "The more I learned, the more I became hooked; biomedical research suddenly started to fascinate me!" Ms. Liu went on to attend the University of Pennsylvania, as part of its Vagelos Scholars Program in Molecular Life Sciences, and is currently pursuing a Ph.D. at Harvard.

Conducting a long-term research project requires diligence, organization and careful planning. This experience will help you develop good work habits and valuable skills that are transferable across academic disciplines and applicable to any line of work. You will likely have teachers to advise you, family to support you; however, you are primarily responsible for the success of your research project. This independence and creative license can be intellectually empowering, but it can also be intimidating, frustrating and tense at times. Obstacles will arise if you challenge yourself—and you should. Learning to anticipate obstacles and stay motivated in the midst of them is excellent preparation for college and beyond. Adam E. Cohen, now Assistant Professor of Chemistry and Chemical Biology at Harvard, began his scientific career in eighth grade, building machines in his New York City bedroom from broken computers and televisions scavenged from the garbage. Cohen learned a tremendous amount by trying to do experiments on his own, "even though I often spent a lot of time barking up the wrong tree." Adam also commented that high school was a particularly good time to be participating in research: "It was very important for me to develop my own scientific aesthetics and interests before I came to college, where I was inundated with other people's ideas. In college I often felt overwhelmed by work, but the memory of what I loved doing in high school helped me keep going. Life got easier after college when I could start working on my own ideas again." Throughout your life, especially during college, your commitment to learning and adapting to new challenges will continually be tested. There is great value in applying yourself to an independent research project, something worthwhile, which interests you. Once you accomplish what you set out to do, you will be able to look back on that experience with pride and satisfaction, and draw upon it when your confidence in yourself may falter.

Unless you are completely invincible and unshakable, you will want to quit at some point during the research process, but you must press on. If you feel like quitting, you should recognize that you are pushing up against your limits. While this is a frustrating feeling, it means that you are growing and you must not quit. Phillip V. Streich, who won numerous awards at ISEF, credited his research experience with making him "more resilient to frustration" and "more comfortable taking risks and making mistakes, ingredients I believe to be the key to creativity and discovery." Persistence in the face of difficult problems is a key attribute of all good scientists, and this trait can help you tackle challenges of any nature. Scientific inquiry demands that the researcher maintain confidence in his or her abilities in the face of setbacks and uncertainty. Comfort with uncertainty is critical to conducting and enjoying one's research. One must cultivate an appreciation for the day-to-day business of research, which is rarely glamorous, and learn to take pleasure in both positive and negative results. An engaging research experience is like mental gymnastics, requiring you to dream up creative experiments that will allow you to investigate a particular question that you are curious about. Research also challenges you to keep your mind open to a wide field of possibilities when interpreting data.

Most successful high school researchers could not have accomplished what they did without the support of their families, mentors, teachers and sponsors. While working independently is critical, learning when and whom to ask for help will also be an important part of your success. Being assertive is a valuable trait to have when conducting research, since you will often need to speak up when you do not understand something or when you have a concern or opinion you want to get across. You will learn how to solicit feedback on your work and how to apply the advice of others to improve your individual efforts. You will have numerous opportunities to develop your written and oral communication skills. You will learn how to present your findings and opinions with integrity, in a fair and balanced way that considers the limitations of your experimental approach and acknowledges alternative interpretations. Depending on your research project, you may learn how to work effectively as part of a team and realize that good teamwork will allow you to achieve results and goals you would not have been able to achieve alone. The sooner you learn these skills, the better, since they will give you an edge in your future endeavors.

Research is also a great way to practice approaching professors and to connect with mentors and role models to inspire and guide you later in life. You will learn how to present yourself and your research in such a way that people will listen and take interest in what you are doing. Alicia Darnell noted that succeeding in science competitions gave her a "voice" with which to present her research to distinguished scientists, "interacting with them as a fellow researcher," as well as to her peers and with the public. Sharing her research with the public was especially significant to Alicia, because it allowed her to help inspire the non-scientific community to support science research. Ms. Darnell's research on Amyotrophic Lateral Sclerosis (ALS) earned her second prize in the Siemens Competition in Math, Science and Technology as well as top honors at the Intel ISEF. Conducting research can be a very empowering experience, since you are investigating questions to which no one knows the answer. You will take the steps necessary to grow as a scientist: you will educate yourself by reading the literature, talking to experts and thinking through what has been done before and what remains to be explored. In so doing, you will hopefully come to realize that your thoughts and ideas are just as interesting and as potentially valuable as anyone else's, even those of a seasoned scientist. Sometimes inexperience can even be an asset, because you will offer a unique perspective and will not feel hindered from taking risks or new approaches to questions and exploring possibilities that previous generations have dismissed as unlikely or untrue. These experiences will embolden you to take on big challenges in the future and to approach them with a positive, strong attitude.

Even as a high school student, research affords you a real opportunity to participate in your chosen field and, possibly, even make a contribution to its progress. What is certain is that you will learn something in the process. You will learn how to ask interesting questions and what it takes to answer them. You will learn something new, that no one has ever known before. You will learn about yourself, what your strengths are and the areas in which you have room to grow. You will learn humility, since the more you know, the more you will realize how much there is left to learn. You will learn that you have something unique to offer the world. You will learn that you can rely on yourself, and you will show others that they can rely on you. You will learn that almost nothing is impossible.

Taking ownership of a research project is a potentially transformative experience, which can give you resilience, confidence and self-sufficiency that will surface in each subsequent project or challenge that you undertake, whether it is academic or personal. By taking advantage of opportunities to present your work whenever you can—at school, regionally, nationally and possibly even internationally—you join a community of researchers united by a zeal for science and driven towards discovery. The company you will keep as part of a research community in high school, college, graduate school and beyond can be fun, enriching and filled with lifelong friendships. Conferences and collaborations can take you across the world and introduce you to an international, diverse group of people, united by a common language and appreciation for science. Embrace these opportunities and try not to be intimidated, because you have nothing to lose (except maybe time and sleep) and a whole world of new perspectives and skills to gain.

In Their Words

"School is a time when your mind is trained, just as an athlete's muscles are trained during practice and exercise. Working on a research project in a scientific or mathematical field will train your mind to think sequentially and carefully, attributes that will help make you successful in any chosen field. Students who avoid science and math often never manage to have rigorous minds, squandering their intellectual gifts because they are unable to properly focus and organize for the task at hand."
Homer Hickam: *Author and Protagonist of October Sky; Gold Medal, National Science Fair*

"Through presentations to Ph.D.s and teachers and peers, I became a confident speaker and developed a sense of pride in my accomplishments. With that personal growth came a desire to share my work with others, and luckily, one of the greatest benefits of succeeding in competitions is the voice your accomplishment gives you."
Alicia Darnell: *Second Place, Siemens Competition; Best of Category in Medicine and Health, Intel International Science and Engineering Fair; National Finalist, Junior Science and Humanities Symposium; Yale Class of 2012*

"Scientific research became my passion and the driving force behind my desire to unravel scientific problems and find innovative solutions. Doing research in high school gave me the confidence that, when I set my mind to it, any challenge can be met."
Franz A. Sauer: *Third Place, National Junior Science and Humanities Symposium; Semifinalist, Siemens Competition; Caltech Class of 2012*

"On a personal level, high school research helped me to become a more outgoing and confident individual; from the many competitions I attended, I learned to remain calm when asked a difficult question, and I grew comfortable speaking to crowds, such as when I presented my project to the public at the National Academy of Sciences via the Intel STS competition."
Chelsea Lynn Jurman: *Fifth Place, Intel Science Talent Search; Third Place, Young Epidemiology Scholars Competition; Yale Class of 2013*

Take-Home Points
• Research, like most things that are worth doing, is not always smooth sailing and will require diligent effort. When you want to give up, keep trying, because you are challenging yourself.

- Do your personal best, but allow for the fact that you are not perfect. Apply yourself and you will reap the benefits of a job well done, which include confidence, resilience, self-sufficiency, communication skills and sophisticated knowledge about your subject.
- Visit the Archimedes Initiative *(www.archimedesinitiative.org)* to see the topical videos, "What I Learned About Myself," "Conquering Fears," and "Teamwork."

3

Scholarships

I'm a firm believer in luck, and I find the harder I work the more of it I have.
Thomas Jefferson

It is becoming increasingly expensive to attend college. Both public and private colleges have raised tuition to almost unprecedented levels, which is making higher education unaffordable to many. That is the bad news. The good news is that there are many scholarships and other forms of financial aid available to diligent students who demonstrate initiative—a quality you clearly possess since you have picked up this book. Merit-based scholarships are awarded by colleges as well as third-party organizations that reward achievements in academics, such as the National Merit Scholarship or the Siemens Award for Advanced Placement, and extracurricular activities, including athletics, public service, debate, mathematics, and, significantly, science and research.

Reasons for Scholarships

Millions of dollars in scholarship money are devoted each year to encouraging high school students to pursue science and research. In fact, some individual awards at scientific competitions are as high as $100,000; therefore, it is possible for you to earn more scholarship money in one science competition than many employees earn in a year of work. Why is this? Large companies that sponsor science competitions, such as Intel and Siemens, are devoted to supporting students entering careers in science and technology in order to promote progress in those fields. Similarly, the government promotes scientific excellence because the economy is driven by research and development. There are serious concerns that the United States is losing its competitive edge to countries like India and China as they begin to produce more innovative researchers and scientists than the United States. To these ends, private companies and the government will keep awarding millions of dollars to promising students who excel in science and research.

Notable Scholarship Opportunities

Many of the following science competitions are described in greater detail in Chapters 16, 17, 18 and 19. This section is meant to whet your appetite by describing some of the scholarships available through participation in these competitions. Apart from scholarship money, expense-paid trips around the country and world are nice bonuses to participating in competitions like ISEF, STS, Siemens, JSHS and others. Many students enter the same research project into each of these competitions, and some do quite well in several. With his invention, the American Sign Language Translator, Ryan Patterson won the top awards at the Intel International Science and Engineering Fair, Intel Science Talent Search, and the Siemens Competition, for well over a total of $250,000 in scholarship money.

Intel International Science and Engineering Fair (ISEF)

Over $4 million dollars in scholarships are disbursed through the annual Intel International Science and Engineering Fair *(http://www.societyforscience. org/isef)* and its hundreds of affiliated fairs around the world. ISEF offers so many awards and scholarships that multiple award ceremonies are required to present them all: Organization Awards, Government Awards and Grand Awards. Organization and Government Awards are known as special awards and usually entail scholarship money, expense-paid trips and other benefits such as free subscriptions to journals and magazines. Scientific organizations (such as the American Chemical Society) and leading companies (such as Google) partner with the ISEF to reward Finalists. The United States government is also fully engaged in sponsoring awards at the ISEF, represented by agencies such as the National Oceanic and Atmospheric Administration, as well as the branches of the military (the Navy, Army, Air Force, and Coast Guard). Colleges such as Drexel University in Philadelphia even offer full-tuition or other significant scholarships to attract top scientific talent to their schools. As for the Grand Awards, over 600 are presented in each of the 18 categories by the Intel ISEF itself. These awards range from $500 for fourth place to $3,000 for first place. If the math does not seem to add up, it is because multiple participants are awarded first, second, third and fourth places. The 18 Best of Category award winners (first place of the first places) receive an additional $5,000 and the top three among them each receive the Intel Foundation Young Scientist Award of $50,000 (as of the 2010 ISEF, two students now receive the Young Scientist Award while one student receives the $75,000 Gordon E. Moore Award). One of the authors of this book, and many of the students quoted within it, have received this top award at the Intel

International Science and Engineering Fair. If that is not enough, there is also the Seaborg SIYSS Award and the European Union Contest for Young Scientists, which respectively entail expense-paid trips to the Nobel Prize ceremonies in Stockholm or the European Union Contest.

Intel Science Talent Search (STS)

Since 1942, the Intel Science Talent Search *(http://www.societyforscience.org/STS)* has been recognizing and awarding scholarships to high school seniors. Each of the 300 semifinalists receives $1,000 and a matching award is given to their schools. The 40 finalists each receive an expense-paid trip to Washington, D.C., and an Intel-powered laptop; additionally, 30 of these finalists receive $7,500. The top ten finalists who place in the competition receive between $20,000 and $100,000 depending upon their placement.

Siemens Competition in Math, Science & Technology

The Siemens Competition *(http://www.siemens-foundation.org/)* is open to individuals in their final year of high school as well as teams of two or three students, each of whom must be in high school. The 300 semifinalists receive Siemens bags containing items such as iPod Shuffles or cameras. The Regional Finalists each receive a $1,000 scholarship and the Regional Winners receive a $3,000 scholarship. National Finalists receive $10,000 to $100,000 depending upon their placement.

Junior Science and Humanities Symposia (JSHS)

The Junior Science and Humanities Symposia program *(http://www.jshs.org/)* is sponsored by the Department of Defense and aims to "prepare and support students to contribute as future scientists and engineers...for the greater good in advancing the nation's scientific and technological progress." The top three regional finalists receive undergraduate tuition scholarships of $2,000, $1,500 and $1,000, and an expense-paid trip to the National JSHS. The top 18 national finalists (first, second or third place in each of six categories) receive scholarships of $12,000, $8,000 and $4,000. Furthermore, the first place winners receive an expense-paid trip to the London International Youth Science Forum.

Davidson Fellows Scholarships

The Davidson Institute for Talent Development *(http://www.davidsongifted.org/Fellows/)* awards scholarships of $50,000, $25,000 and $10,000 to "extraordinary young people under the age of 18 who have completed a significant piece of work" in the categories of mathematics, science, literature, music, technology, philosophy and "outside the box." These scholarships often go to high school students who have shown promise by completing significant research projects.

Young Epidemiology Scholars (YES) Competition

The Young Epidemiology Scholars Competition *(http://www.collegeboard.com/yes/)* is sponsored by the College Board and the Robert Wood Johnson Foundation. According to their website, each year up to 120 high school juniors and seniors who conduct outstanding research projects that apply epidemiological methods of analysis to a health-related issue share as much as $456,000 in college scholarships. Up to 60 semifinalists receive $1,000 and 60 regional finalists receive expense-paid trips to Washington, D.C., to compete in the regional and national finals. Of these regional finalists, 48 receive $2,000 each, six receive $15,000 each, two receive $20,000 each, two receive $35,000 each and two more receive $50,000 each.

College-Based Scholarships

As mentioned above, some colleges partner with competitions like ISEF to offer tuition scholarships to high school scientists. More often, colleges offer their own merit scholarships which they award to students who have demonstrated initiative and achievement, often through high school research projects. A good example is that of the A.B. Duke Memorial Scholarship, which provides full funding to attend Duke University, and is often given to students who have engaged significantly in research. There are countless other examples of college scholarships that are awarded to high school researchers.

> "There are certainly several glittery benefits to completing a successful research project in high school. With polished presentation skills and someone to make sure you know your project is on a near-graduate level, earning generous amounts of scholarship money from the bigger science competitions is quite possible."
> **Alicia Darnell**: *Second Place, Siemens Competition; Best of Category in Medicine and Health, Intel International Science and Engineering Fair; National Finalist, Junior Science and Humanities Symposium; Yale Class of 2012*

> "From doing research, I received the amazing opportunity to attend science fairs such as ISEF and win money to continue to fund my research as well as scholarship money for college."
> **Wendy Zhang**: *Finalist, Intel International Science and Engineering Fair*

Take-Home Points

- Millions of dollars of scholarship money are awarded to high school researchers each year.
- There are many competitions that award up to $100,000 to top winners and substantial amounts to finalists and semifinalists.
- Colleges frequently offer merit-based scholarships to students who have done high school research because these students have demonstrated initiative and achievement.

4

College Admissions

Quite honestly I don't think I would have gotten into the colleges that I got into without my high school research experience. I was blessed and fortunate to have done well in several national and international science competitions but beyond that I think many admissions committees look to research as a sign that a student is willing to work hard and wants to do something beyond traditional textbook learning. It shows initiative and drive and I think that those are qualities in which top colleges are interested.

Arun Thottumkara: *Second Place, Siemens Competition; First Place, National Junior Science and Humanities Symposium; Semifinalist, Intel Science Talent Search; Best of Category in Chemistry, Intel International Science and Engineering Fair; Harvard Class of 2008*

Although most high school researchers do not win thousands of dollars through their research, they still have a significant edge over other students because they demonstrated their ability to complete a significant piece of work. Many colleges have their own merit-based scholarships that they award to these students. Additionally, unlike many of their peers, research students can often receive impressive recommendations from faculty mentors who work at universities.

In Their Words

Note that while many of these research students have had success with the college application process, research experiences or awards are not guarantees that one will be accepted. Colleges often look for driven students who may be able to contribute to their campuses; research is often a great venue to demonstrate this potential. Additionally, many of the student researchers quoted below chose to attend "top colleges" as judged by the strength and breadth of their research programs; there are many other colleges that have focused and equally strong research opportunities.

> "My success in competitions has contributed to my acceptance at top colleges including Yale University, Harvard University and Princeton University, but I believe that the experiences associated with the research and competitions have been just as critical to my admittance: the way these experiences have shaped me overall as a person has likely made me a stronger applicant."
>
> **Lauren R. Lisann**: *Finalist, Intel Science Talent Search; Semifinalist, Siemens Competition; Winner, American Academy of Neurology Neuroscience Research Prize; Yale Class of 2012*

"Winning Siemens almost certainly [helped me gain admission] to Harvard and MIT"
Yin Li: *First Place, Siemens Competition; Finalist, Intel International Science and Engineering Fair; Harvard Class of 2008*

"It goes without saying, then, that the prestige and respect gained from success in science research may earn you a coveted spot at [top colleges]."
Alicia Darnell: *Second Place, Siemens Competition; Best of Category in Medicine and Health, Intel International Science and Engineering Fair; National Finalist, Junior Science and Humanities Symposium; Yale Class of 2012*

"The main benefit of doing research in high school for me was that I got into great colleges! I was definitely helped in college admissions by being a Siemens regional finalist. I got into every college I applied to: Harvard, Yale, Princeton, Duke, UNC Chapel Hill."
Amanda R. Mason: *Regional Finalist, Siemens Competition; Regional Finalist, Junior Science and Humanities Symposium; Harvard Class of 2009*

"I would absolutely say that my research in high school prepared me for college more than any other program, activity or class in which I participated. The high standards and importance of self-paced, independent work are so important not only in college, but in today's competitive job market, where one must always go "above and beyond." I do think that my research helped me to get accepted into Barnard (and pay for it), as this kind of unique program makes any application stand out. It shows colleges that you have already done work on their level and could be a great asset to their labs or other programs."
Ilana Rice: *Second Place, Young Epidemiology Scholars Competition; Finalist, Junior Science and Humanities Symposium; Semifinalist, Intel Science Talent Search; Barnard Class of 2013*

It has become increasingly difficult to gain admission into college, let alone the top colleges. This is largely due to the rising number and quality of applicants. The growing competitiveness has resulted in the establishment of an entire industry of college admission counselors. Students are investing thousands of dollars towards college admissions—money that they hope will translate into acceptance letters. However, without any tangible content, such as academic achievements or extracurricular activities, a student stands little chance of acceptance, regardless of how much money he or she spends to make his or her application more attractive. An application without unique accomplishments is analogous to a hamburger without any meat: although it looks appetizing at first, when an admissions officer bites into it he or she is disappointed. Their application is analogous to a hamburger without any meat: though it looks appetizing, when an admissions officer bites into it he or she is disappointed. Fortunately, research is a great way not only to develop as a person, but to "add meat" to your résumé and look more appealing to colleges.

Why Do Colleges Care About Research?

"Harvard College has long sought to enroll students who will take advantage of the rich academic opportunities available here and certainly students involved in research can demonstrate their academic interests and enthusiasm through their projects. Some high school students pursue research outside of their regular course work; others approach class projects, labs or term papers as opportunities to hone research skills and delve deeply into an area of interest. Students with compelling examples of research can include them with their applications, and our admissions officers may in turn pass exceptional pieces on to our faculty members for evaluation and feedback."

William R. Fitzsimmons: *Dean of Admissions and Financial Aid at Harvard College*

Admissions officers and their staff read through tens of thousands of applications every year. Thousands of students have perfect or near-perfect grade point averages; hundreds are valedictorians or have perfect SAT scores, and many are athletes, musicians or student leaders. These are not insignificant achievements and should not be downplayed, but colleges often have to make admissions decision using simple economics: supply and demand. Keep in mind that this is a loose analogy that basically explains that the rarer something is the more perceived value it has. Students constitute the "supply" while colleges are the "buyers." The larger the supply of a given type of student, the less the colleges demand it. However, by doing research you can move into the more elite supply curve with far fewer students: those who have done research, possibly achieved recognition at large competitions, and, at the pinnacle, even published their research in an academic journal. Colleges thus have a built-in method to recruit students actually interested in research since it is unlikely for someone who just wants to use research as a college admissions tool to accomplish these things.

But why do colleges want students who do research in the first place? Research shows independent motivation and the ability to carry an idea through completion. Colleges like to recruit these motivated students because they have clearly demonstrated their innovativeness as well as their perseverance—two qualities that they hope will carry with the student into their colleges. College professors are often looking for bright, motivated students who can help with their research. Many undergraduate-initiated research projects lead to exciting avenues of research and publications—a win-win situation for professors and students alike. Even if the student decides not to do research in college, he or she will use the aforementioned qualities to make contributions in other fields and bring recognition to the college. Once you realize that colleges stand to benefit from your matriculation (as a motivated research student) just as much as you stand to benefit from their acceptance, you will feel much more secure about your application.

The College Application

The college application is a daunting process for most high school students. Among the most important aspects of the application are recommendations, essays and the interview. Fortunately, research experience will give you an edge in all three of these areas. Research opens up a built-in support system consisting of thousands of former high school research students who got into top colleges. At competitions like ISEF it is common to meet other research students older than you who are applying to, or who have already have gotten into, the colleges of their choice. Many are willing to share advice on colleges and the application process when it comes time for you to apply. Some may even offer their dorm rooms as a place to stay when you visit. Why? Their predecessors helped them, just as you will help your successors when you are in college. Indeed, the guide that you are reading is a culmination of advice from some of the most helpful and knowledgeable students from the research world.

Recommendations

> "We view research-related activities favorably. How favorably depends on the nature of the research and the depth of student engagement over time. For evaluation purposes, it helps us to have a letter from the student's primary research mentor."
> **Jeffrey Brenzel**: *Dean of Undergraduate Admissions at Yale University*

Recommendation letters are one of the most important components of a college application because they give the college a third party's perspective on the student. Most students are only able to ask their high school teachers or employers to write recommendations. By doing research at a university while in high school (and impressing your mentor sufficiently, see Chapter 9: Impressing your Mentor), you can get an excellent recommendation not only from your high school teacher, but from a research professor as well. This significantly adds weight to your application because a college professor is vouching for your ability to succeed at your desired college. Your mentor most likely has taught college students and knows what types of students do well. You are one of these students; so let your professor tell the admissions officer that. Additionally, doing well at high school research can allow you to meet and impress other potential recommendation writers: directors of summer programs, principals or superintendents of your school system and company representatives (e.g., Siemens or Intel). Your high school teacher may also be able to write an even more outstanding recommendation after your research experience because many research competitions provide awards or expense-paid travel for you and your high school teacher—imagine the ebullient recommendation letter your high school teacher will write after he or she travels on an expense-paid trip with you! When requesting a letter of recommendation from your teacher or professor, it is important to ask them to stress your commitment to and enthusiasm for the research, and to cite specific examples. It is better for them to provide tangible stories as examples of your qualities rather than to write generally. Recommendations based off of your project will go a long way in impressing college admissions officers.

Essays

Another major aspect of your college application is the essay. It is arguably the most important (and potentially frustrating) essay you will write in high school. Students have spent many nights struggling over what they can write to convey why they would be a good fit for a particular college. Again, students who did research in high school have an edge. It is relatively easy for them to describe their research experience as the most significant activity of their high school career (often it is!) because they have explained this a million times before to judges at competitions. Given your previous experience doing research, it is clear that you will be able to contribute to the college by working with a professor on a research project. Often, a good idea is to list one or two professors at the college whose research interests you and who you may consider contacting even before you submit your application. This demonstrates that you truly have taken an interest in that college in particular. In addition, the résumé of a high school research student often speaks for itself. It is very impressive to include your research experience in your college application essays by listing which institution you worked at, who you worked under, what you did (briefly), how long you worked there and any recognition you received.

Interviews

Though a less important part of your application due to its subjectivity, the interview is still something that can work heavily in your favor. Interviews are usually just conversations about topics such as your interests, activities and goals for college. Research students shine during this process as they can describe with enthusiasm the research they did in high school. Many high school students who have done medical research know more about cutting-edge fields like stem cell research than their interviewers. It is very impressive if you can really show enthusiasm for what you've done, as well as teach your interviewer something about your field.

Conclusion

Clearly, one of the residual benefits of doing research is increasing your chances of getting into the college of your choice. It is important, however, that you do not do research because "it will look good on a college application." Research, like any other activity, requires passion and enthusiasm to be successful. If it appears that you did research solely for college admissions purposes it may harm, rather than help, your application. However, if you are truly passionate about research and heed the advice in the following chapters, then you stand to benefit greatly.

Take-Home Points

- High school research can increase your chance of being accepted by the colleges of your choice.
- A recommendation from your research mentor can give you an edge over other applicants.
- Your research project gives you a natural topic to write about in your admissions essay or discuss during your college interview.

5

Career Decisions

"The exposure to a real research environment also gives students insight into research as a career and makes them more mindful of their long-term interests and aspirations."
Leslie Beh: *Best of Category in Microbiology, Intel International Science and Engineering Fair; Research Science Institute; Harvard Class of 2011*

"This research experience definitely led me to my choice of major and minor, and even what college I would attend. I hope to become a professor and continue research for the rest of my life, working in the field of behavioral ecology and aiding international conservation efforts."
Alexis Mychajliw: *Finalist, Intel Science Talent Search; Cornell Class of 2012*

"A high school and even college student interested in science and unfamiliar with research is unlikely to have much of any idea of what life as a scientist is like and jump into a science major completely unaware. High school research, hopefully in one's field of interest (as I did with astrophysics), allows one to go to college with a much better idea of what it is like to be a research scientist, what it is like to be in that particular field day-to-day, and ultimately whether that is a career worth pursuing. Even for the student who does research and drops science there are experiences and skills learned that are well and important, but this 'testing the waters' for future scientists is unbelievably important."
Adam Solomon: *Third Place, Siemens Competition; Eighth Place, Intel Science Talent Search; Yale Class of 2010*

Research experiences as early as high school can shape one's career decisions. Some may have wonderful times in the laboratory and will choose to pursue a research career; others may realize they want to pursue something else in college and beyond. This *Guide* aims to help you get a proper research experience so you can make an educated decision about what you pursue in college and possibly post graduation.

Deciding Upon Careers

Clearly, as a reader of this *Guide* to *high school* research, you have a lot of time to decide upon your future career. You may be happy to know the options are wide open to you, especially given the résumé that you have begun building by picking up this *Guide*. It is quite common for researchers to have job mobility, many moving between academia and industry. Successful high school researchers often say that the early exposure to research careers confirmed their interests in careers in professional science or related fields. These high school researchers are immersed in an academic environment with a principal investigator (PI) and postdoctoral, doctoral, graduate and undergraduate students so they quickly learn how research groups operate. Many high schools have "career-shadowing" programs; research can be considered as a more active and substantial "shadowing" process. High school students are eyewitnesses to, or even participants in, the writing of scientific papers for journals, presentations at professional conferences, composition of grant submissions and other professional activities. This exposure, as one former Siemens Competition National Winner put it, allowed him to "hit the ground running" towards his career goals when he entered college.

By no means does every high school researcher become a college professor. As mentioned previously, research can at times be extremely rewarding but also very frustrating. It is uncommon, if not impossible, for a true researcher to experience one without the other (like spin-paired electrons, the positive is accompanied by the negative). Many students are motivated to continue research throughout college and beyond by their experiences in high school; others decide they are interested in other disciplines. In fact, at Harvard, there are a great number of students who enjoyed research success in high school but decided to switch to economics (the most popular major at Harvard), with an eye towards banking or consulting, by their sophomore year. It is not uncommon for research Ph.D.s also to switch from science to finance or other fields. Though many were former bench scientists, their transitions were relatively smooth because their research experiences primed them for success in other fields. The method by which scientists solve questions (also known as the 'Scientific Method') can be effectively applied to any number of other fields. Analytical and problem-solving skills are critical in most professional careers, so starting research in high school is a good way to develop these early.

Types of Careers in Which Researchers Thrive

Academia

Many very successful professors have cherished their research experiences at every step of the ladder—high school, college, graduate school, post-doctoral fellowship and eventually tenured professor. Indeed, the Science Talent Search has a list of former finalists who went on to win Nobel Prizes, Fields Medals, MacArthur Fellowships ("genius grants") or election to the National Academy of Science, among other honors. Though these scientists' later successes may not be solely attributable to their research in high school, it is very likely that the seeds of their careers were planted in high school. Indeed, Leroy Hood who is famous for inventing "four instruments that have unlocked much of the mystery of human biology," such as the automated DNA sequencer as well as synthesizer, started his research career as a high school student and even participated in the 1956 Westinghouse Science Talent Search. He said, "My high school research experience was seminal in giving me an understanding of what science really was and the kind of people who practice science." Research presents opportunities to attend top research universities and interact with pioneers or even creators, of fields that may interest you. This direct exposure to cutting-edge research can certainly give one an edge when applying to graduate schools and formulating a thesis idea or research focus.

Industry

Like the aforementioned professors, many CEOs and Chief Scientific Officers (CSOs) of Research & Development (R & D) companies developed their scientific interests in high school and college. Their goal transitioned from answering a specific research question to actually applying research through an entrepreneurial venture. Amazingly, some high school researchers gain their first business experience while *in high school!* Each year about 20 percent of ISEF finalists are in the process of filing or already have filed a patent. Some have even started their own companies. For example, Philip Streich, who received Third Place at the 2008 Intel Science Talent Search and won the 2007 ISEF Young Scientist Award, co-founded a company called Graphene Solutions that manufactures carbon nanotubes and won the Wisconsin Governor's Business Plan award. His research also has given him experience working with patent attorneys and "writing and submitting multiple patent disclosures and licenses to the University of Wisconsin." Clearly, the experience of filing patents and starting companies based on high school research are unparalleled if one wants to go into a career in industry.

Journalism

Scientists must be able to convey complex ideas in simple prose if they are to attract funding or attention to their research. This is a skill that high school researchers develop when they submit papers or give presentations to general audiences at competitions. This also happens to be an important skill for journalists, scientific or not. Students may decide that they are really interested in communicating profound and complicated ideas or discoveries to the public. Researchers who can write clearly and concisely are able to write for a broad variety of publications, ranging from *Nature* to *Scientific American* to *Time*. Fortunately, in most colleges there are a number of publications, including science magazines, which one can join to develop their journalistic skills. These include small, campus-based journals as well as large, established journals such as the *Journal of Young Investigators (www.jyi.org)*.

Medicine

Medical professionals need to solve research questions on a daily basis. They have to use the basic scientific method to treat patients: posing a question, proposing a hypothesis, doing the experiment, analyzing the result and drawing conclusions. For example, an elderly patient comes in with a wet cough and reports being easily fatigued. The former high school researcher-turned-medical doctor asks him- or herself, "Why does the patient have a wet cough? My hypothesis is that the cough is due to the patient's recent myocardial infarction (heart attack). Let me try increasing the pumping power of the left ventricle to decrease the amount of fluid backed up in the pulmonary circuit. Did this work? If not, what other theories are there? If it did, let me write up the report, prescribe treatment and discharge the patient." This is clearly a contrived and hypothetical scenario, but the point is the same nonetheless.

At high school research competitions, such as ISEF, one of the most popular categories is medicine because many of the students are aspiring doctors and/or medical researchers. It is intensely gratifying for one's research to be applied in a way that directly helps people. Fortunately for patients everywhere, some pretty bright high school researchers may be their doctors in the near future.

> "...research has driven me to pursue a career in the field of medicine or become a research scientist. My dream job would be to work as a researcher at the CDC in Atlanta, Georgia."
> **Natalie Saranga Omattage**: *Intel Foundation Young Scientist, Intel International Science and Engineering Fair; Semifinalist, Siemens Competition; University of Richmond Class of 2012*

Business

Analytical thinking skills are crucial in business. Indeed some of the most successful Wall Street investment firms specifically recruit students who did research in high school and college. These companies include prestigious firms like D.E. Shaw, which is known for its accomplished team (ranging from science competition winners to chess champions to physicists-turned-financial analysts). Investment banking requires the ability to carry out a project through completion and to think creatively about options—two characteristics that research helps develop. In addition to banking, Venture Capital (VC) firms also have a need for research insiders. A great amount of VC funding is going into start-up research companies in hot fields such as nanotechnology, genetics and stem cell research. These VC firms need bright young people who are familiar with the research areas that the firm may be investing in. Research experience gives these people a distinct advantage because, even if the research one does is not in the specific field that the VC firm is interested in, he or she knows how to read scientific papers analytically. This allows the company to distinguish between solid science that should be funded and hype that should not.

Networking

One invaluable benefit high school students overlook is meeting people at all stages of their careers. Science competitions and summer camps thrust you into environments where you make friendships and professional contacts without even realizing it. Many high school researchers have said they met their best friends at summer programs like the Research Science Institute (RSI) or competitions like Intel Science Talent Search (STS). Though this may seem like too short a period to forge such strong friendships, it is less surprising when one considers a secondary goal of these programs. They bring together students who share two fundamental qualities—a passion for science and an insatiable curiosity. Oftentimes high school students with these interests do not meet similar people until college or even later in life; however, within one day of attending the International Science and Engineering Fair, for example, they are exposed to over a thousand other students who are equally interested in research and discovery. Many of these science fair participants will matriculate into the same colleges (in fact, schools like MIT have an annual reception at ISEF) and pursue similar majors, so it is easy to see how a brief meeting at a competition can turn into a long-term friendship.

Science fairs also help students meet and form connections with professionals at various stages of their careers—also known as judges. While the majority of judges are professors and scientists, and all have Ph.D.s or the equivalent, many judges come from non-research professions. Some are doctors and businessmen; others are engineers and journalists. It is common for these judges or company representatives to give you their business cards and ask you to contact them. Do not be hesitant to ask them if there is a way for you to contact them, especially if you had an interesting conversation. These people are often helpful and can give you career advice, recommend you to scholarships offered by their company, introduce you to their contacts or even set up internships for you.

> "Doing high school research projects expanded my intellectual vitality. I learned what it means to be a prospective scientist. From my experiences, I realized that I would someday like to become a university professor and researcher in astronomy. Through working on my projects and presenting at various competitions, I also met many individuals, students and professionals alike, who share my passion for science. Perhaps getting to know science-oriented peers, some of whom became my good friends, was the greatest reward. It created a sense of community I did not know before."
>
> **Philip Mocz**: *Eighth Place, Intel Science Talent Search; Second Place Team, Siemens Competition; Finalist, Intel International Science and Engineering Fair; Finalist, Junior Science and Humanities Symposium; Harvard Class of 2012*

These are just a few examples of careers in which researchers can be found. Consider yourself in good company!

Take-Home Points

- Research experiences can help you decide upon your college major and even future career.
- There are many careers in which researchers thrive, including academia, industry, journalism, medicine and business.
- Visit the Archimedes Initiative *(www.archimedesinitiative.org)* to see the topical video, "Preparing for the Future."

Part II:
Getting Started on a Project

6

Formulating an Idea

The best way to have a good idea is to have a lot of ideas.
Linus Pauling

Introduction

Formulating a research idea is not a one-time effort, but rather a continuous process. Inevitably, an initial idea develops over time as research takes unexpected turns, gains complexity and becomes more specific. Sometimes, an exciting first thought leads to a dead end, such as a concept already widely established or previously discredited. In such cases, you need to either restart the process of searching for an idea or find interesting wrinkles of uncertainty in the topic at hand. It is important not to become frustrated or discouraged if you do not strike gold during the first attempt. Usually, the best ideas are those that are carefully developed over time. Fortunately, the very process of probing a topic familiarizes you with the terrain of knowledge through which you have to navigate, regardless of the eventual outcome. When you finally encounter an idea, its sophistication will reflect the great amount of thought you have invested. Ultimately, the key to formulating a great project idea is to *start thinking about it early*.

Passion, Research and Communication

The process of hunting for an idea varies from person to person and from discipline to discipline. Some students spend days in libraries absorbing a plethora of information from a variety of fields; others delve into a topic already presented to them by a mentor; and there are also a few (especially mathematicians) who just sit and think. Unfortunately, there is no single protocol that prescribes steps A, B and C to arrive at a fabulous idea D.

Despite these differences, however, all great idea searches share commonalities that are integral to the strength, allure and promise of a concocted research topic. These commonalities are *passion, background research* and *communication*.

This chapter will elaborate on these three components of formulating an idea and will offer a general approach that can maximize your chances of finding a research topic that both resonates with your passions and holds great potential to evolve into a meaningful and award-winning research endeavor.

Passion: Starting in the Right Direction

Successful research results when you take ownership of an idea that you are genuinely passionate about. The degree of your interest in the project topic determines the amount of personal investment you will allocate to the project throughout your research journey—the more investment, the more initiative you will take to explore the topic and the better your project will become.

Turning on Your Interest Radar

Though the majority of students do this automatically when they look for a research idea, it is never too much to stress the importance of choosing an idea in a field that motivates you to explore and discover. It is not enough to settle on a topic that you think will win the science fair if you do not have an intellectual attachment to it. Though some students find rewarding ideas by randomly browsing papers and books across various scientific disciplines, most of those who triumph in higher-level science fairs and other competitions start with well-defined interests in mind.

Instead of going out of your way to scavenge for ideas and overwhelming yourself with old science books and publications—in fact, before you start doing anything—*think*. Think about the science topics that give you goose bumps of excitement, that make you say "Wow!", and that entice you to find out more about them. What areas in science compel you to read, watch and listen further without being prompted by class requirements or by your teachers?

Some students have difficulty identifying specific science topics in which they are especially interested. They love science in general. Every aspiring scientist, however, is partial to certain areas, even if he or she does not realize it. All that is required to uncover hidden passions is a simple systematic introspection.

Practically, this means becoming more aware of how the choices you have made and are currently making dictate your scientific preferences—in short, turning on your *personal interest radar*. Conscientiously scan for traces of evidence in your daily life that hint at distinct fields of interest. Make note of the science books you read, your favorite science classes, the science-oriented activities you enjoy, the Discovery or Science Channel shows that grab your attention, and even your future career aspirations. Carefully ponder your life up to now: which science topics absorb you the most? Furthermore, ask yourself why you are interested in these topics. Do you hope to cure a disease, alleviate the world's energy crisis, understand the origin of the universe or rationalize patterns of human behavior? Only by unearthing the roots of your interests can you be truly motivated to pursue research.

Note: Even though considering your future career goals can help you pin down your scientific passions, do not be constrained by them. It is perfectly fine for your science interests to deviate from your intended future career (which may change with time). For example, just because you want to be a doctor does not mean you need to work in a molecular biology lab (though, as was mentioned in an earlier chapter, research experience can help you decide upon your future career). What matters now is sifting through your daily activities and interests to find your true scientific passion(s).

> "I've always been interested in animal behavior and the delicate interplay between environment and ecological function. I have been fortunate enough to have spent all of my summers in the Catskill Mountains of upstate New York. My father and aunt encouraged my adventures into the forests, and would even aid me in my early specimen collection (frogs, newts, bugs and the like). I never called these outings a "science," but after taking several high school science classes and realizing that a laboratory course of study did not pique my interest, I went back to doing what I know."
> **Alexis Mychajliw**: *Finalist, Intel Science Talent Search; Cornell Class of 2012*

> "I believe students should first select their major area of the investigation (i.e., heredity, alternate fuels, molecular biology, informatics, etc.). We then discuss what they can possibly do given their interests, academic backgrounds, knowledge, time commitments, available equipment, etc. I have found over the years that when I make the initial suggestion (because I find the topic very interesting) very often the student will lose interest in the topic because it wasn't their area of interest from day one."
> **Nevin E. Longenecker**: *Veteran Research Teacher and creator of the Research Program at Johns Adams High School in South Bend, Indiana*

Fine-tuning Your Interest Radar

Once you are confident about your selected field(s) of interest, narrow down your preferences to particular topics and subfields. If you are interested in cancer research, what exactly is it about cancer that fascinates you? Molecular defects in the cell cycle? Genetic profiling? Drug screening? You may not have reached a stage where you can specify in detail the research that you want to pursue. In this case, try to recall and search for the cutting-edge topics in your field(s). Most importantly, go to online databases of research institutions such as the National Institutes of Health, the Howard Hughes Medical Institute, NASA, the Max Planck Institute and university research departments. On those websites, search for your general fields of interest and browse through each lab's research in the field to narrow down topics and spark new ideas. The wealth of ongoing research at these institutions provides a panoramic view of the leading research efforts in your fields of interest. These databases give you a sense of the big and small questions scientists are currently tackling, and will help you orient yourself in the vast, interweaving tapestry of the field so that you can make informed decisions about your eventual research focus.

> "I became very interested in human behavior after learning about game theory in AP microeconomics. I had also read Richard Thaler's *The Winner's Curse* and Stephan Meier's *Economics of Non-Selfish Behaviour* and was curious as to why people donate money, a seemingly irrational action in the world of economics. I wanted to apply the different theories of why people donate to the real world, and chose to look at donation behavior in the context of public libraries..."
> **Xiaomeng Zeng**: *Finalist, Intel Science Talent Search; Harvard Class of 2012*

Background Research: Foundations for Your Central Question

Regardless of whether you narrowed down your specific research topics through the steps above or whether a mentor provided you with an idea to start with, background research is indispensable for you to take ownership of your work and generate your own questions. If you followed the advice above, then you already have a good start on background research. The purpose of background research is to identify *gaps in knowledge, unanswered questions* or *contested theories* for you to investigate in your own novel project. Your goal at this stage is not yet to become an expert in a given research topic. Technical language will present a barrier to your full understanding, but you do not need to understand every unfamiliar term to apprehend the big picture.

Zoning in on Radar Targets

Returning to the interest radar analogy, the next thing you have to do after selecting your research focus is to recognize and target the central question(s) you want to tackle in your project. The best way to approach this is to read background material with a critical mind. Just like reading the passages on the SAT or ACT, read actively by summarizing main points and asking questions (indeed, doing background research may actually help you perform better on critical reading sections of these standardized tests). Enumerate the knowns and the unknowns of a topic. What is missing in the puzzle? What is confusing to you? What are scientists trying to *answer, explain* or *support*?

The questions you ask during your background research contribute to the process of formulating project ideas in two ways. First, mentally probing the information strengthens your curiosity about the topic, thus motivating you to research more and generate more questions. Second, the very questions you formulate now can potentially become the central question, the impetus of your research. Do not yet concern yourself about the feasibility or possibility of answering the questions, and avoid discarding your questions prematurely. Presently, the focus is to engage your mind and to ask as many questions as you can. Always record your questions and ideas immediately after you think about them.

Finally, do not merely understand the reading. *Synthesize* it. Like completing a jigsaw puzzle, piece together diverse perspectives and ideas from different sources and build a comprehensive picture of the topic. Play around with the information available: Look for parts that do not fit, parts that contradict each other. Develop your own thoughts, hypotheses and explanations about a problem within a reasonable context. Immerse yourself in the topic while examining it from many different angles.

> "Doing background research on ALS, I noticed an unanswered question in published papers. There had been several suggestions implicating a splicing defect in ALS pathogenesis, but definitive data had never been obtained in genetically affected mice or humans. Based on these suggestions...I decided to search for a splicing defect in gene targets of the splicing regulator Nova, an RNA binding protein that is targeted in human motor disease."
> **Alicia Darnell**: *Second Place, Siemens Competition; Best of Category in Medicine and Health, Intel International Science and Engineering Fair; National Finalist, Junior Science and Humanities Symposium; Yale Class of 2012*

Sources for Background Research

One of the most popular repositories for general knowledge is Wikipedia. While you should never take the content on Wikipedia for granted, the online (and universally editable) encyclopedia can serve as a first stop in your background research. Generally, articles in Wikipedia highlight the most important aspects of a topic while providing a concise overview of the topic as a whole. Use Wikipedia to familiarize yourself with the field the first time around and allow the information presented to prompt questions so that you can look further into the content in other, more reliable, sources. An additional use of Wikipedia is the list of sources at the bottom of the page, which can direct you to journal articles, books and other websites. Such references can be very useful, especially when you do not know where to start your background research.

Most of your scientific research however, should be based on articles and papers in peer-reviewed journals and scientific magazines. These publications provide reliable and current reports of top-notch research happening around the world and serve as archives for significant work done in the past. If your topic belongs to biology, chemistry, psychology or related fields then PubMed *(http://www.ncbi.nlm.nih.gov/pubmed/)*, a publications search engine maintained by the U.S. National Library of Medicine, is an essential research tool. For other fields in science (biology as well), well-known journals such as *Nature, Science* and the *Proceedings of the National Academy of Sciences (PNAS)* showcase the leading national and international research efforts across all disciplines. If you want a summary and an evaluation of the pivotal research advances accomplished over the years in a certain field, then review journals such as the Nature Reviews are quite useful. For a lay explanation of scientific advances, popular science magazines such as *Scientific American* and *Popular Science* offer clarifying insights into otherwise complex subjects. Even Dr. Leroy Hood, who is famous for inventing the automated DNA sequencer among other valuable devices, credits a 1956 article in Scientific American with piquing his interest in molecular biology (that same year, he competed in the Westinghouse Science Talent Search). Beyond abstracts, full access to articles published in these journals unfortunately requires subscription. Generally, libraries and even some schools subscribe to these journals and make them available to their members, so ask around for people and places that can help you gain access to such a wealth of information.

> "After my mentor gave me a protein to work with and a technique with which to analyze it, I spent many hours on PubMed reading essentially and tangentially related papers and thinking about how they fit together. I kept my preliminary results at the back of my mind, and eventually started to relate them to observations in the literature."
> **Kelley Harris**: *Third Place, Intel Science Talent Search; Semifinalist, Siemens Competition; Harvard Class of 2009*

Communication: Shaping and Polishing Your Ideas

Since science research is highly collaborative, formulating great ideas requires exchanges among scientists. Communication with researchers who are experts in your field of interest can provide valuable insights into your ideas.

One of the crucial steps that many students overlook in formulating project ideas is discussing them with peers and experts in the field. There is no danger in jeopardizing the authorship of your idea while communicating it to someone else. In fact, you probably formulated your ideas by reading other peoples' thoughts presented in the publications you have read, so talking with another person is merely an extension of the intellectual exchange that is so fundamental to developing project ideas.

Also, there is no need to fear that your thoughts and opinions might sound foolish and inadequate to an accomplished scientist. First of all, no one expects high school students to possess the same amount of knowledge of a field as researchers with years of experience. Secondly, proposing your own views and asking questions about a complex research problem show that you have properly thought about the problem.

When talking to a mentor or another scientist, there is no need to have a concrete idea in mind. Having a firmer grasp of the progress and advances of a certain type of research, a professional research scientist can often direct you to current problems and questions in the field. In most cases, this is what happens: A student finds a mentor in a lab whose research the student is interested in. The mentor and the student discuss possible projects, after which the mentor suggests a problem for the student to explore. It is then up to the student to take the initiative to formulate hypotheses and ideas about the problem.

This does not mean that you should look for a mentor to spoon-feed you with a project topic. Keep in mind that ultimately your own investment and passion toward the research you do will determine your project's success. Therefore, be sure that you have done background research before contacting a scientist. This will foster a two-way exchange of ideas rather than a meeting in which somebody else tells you what you should do for research. If you meet the scientist in person, always have a piece of paper and pen ready to record insights and information that will help you. Finally, ask for supplemental reading material regarding the topic of discussion. The expert has a better notion of the information that is most representative of the field and most appropriate to engage the thoughts of a novice.

Conversations with experts are an invaluable opportunity for you to further develop your ideas and gain helpful advice from experienced researchers.

> "Once I'd extended some old questions into questions about my own results, I talked to my research advisor about the connections I was seeing and what I wanted to know about my proteins. She helped me design an experiment that would provide some answers."
> **Kelley Harris:** *Third Place, Intel Science Talent Search; Semifinalist, Siemens Competition; Harvard Class of 2009*

The Serendipity of Accidental Ideas: Being Observant, Alert and Inquisitive

In the fields of observation chance favors only the prepared mind.
Louis Pasteur

From time to time, magnificent ideas spring from fortuitous events that occur in the right place at the right time. In fact, many seminal discoveries in science (such as the discoveries of penicillin and carbon nanotubes) were results of unintended consequences of carefully designed experiments. Though some attribute these ideas and discoveries to pure luck, much more than luck is involved in transforming these accidents into scientific advances.

Accidental scientific epiphanies are certainly not born out of a vacuum. Scientists do not idle around waiting for an idea to form spontaneously. Rather, ideas form through a process similar to that which created the first amino acids (according to the seminal experiment by Miller and Urey); the conditions had to be right for the chance electrical discharge to create the complex structures. Scientific "accidents," therefore, are not really accidents at all, but additional sharp observations that yield novel and different insights about a subject. Without the knowledge and the alertness to recognize peripheral or unintended results as important manifestations of science, you cannot transform an accident into a visionary idea or discovery even if it could be the most important finding in the history of science.

Accidental ideas are rare, so you should not rely upon the gift of chance, but when they occur, they tend to be the most exciting and ground-breaking of all. Therefore, it is important in your process of developing, polishing and testing your ideas to keep an open mind, and always be alert, observant and inquisitive about your research environment. These qualities compose the mental net that catches the fortunate accidents that can slip away unnoticed by an inattentive problem solver.

> "I was using thin-layer chromatography to track the progress of a reaction. I took some pictures of the TLC plates to put on my display board. When I printed the pictures, I accidentally pushed a button in Photoshop and one of the chemical spots turned blue and the rest stayed black...I learned later that this button emphasized colors that the camera could see, but my eyes could not. When searching for my next research project, I thought back to the weird incident and tried to figure out what it might mean. After doing some quick experiments, I realized that the chemical I was studying was fluorescent and the TLC plates were so much brighter than the chemical spot that my eyes could not see it, only the camera picked up on it. I started studying more fluorescent chemicals to see if I could detect the fluorescence with a digital camera. This formed the qualitative aspect of my project—I discovered that digital photography could help identify some chemicals on a TLC plate."
> **Amber Hess:** *First Place in Chemistry, Intel International Science and Engineering Fair; Finalist, Intel Science Talent Search; Semifinalist, Siemens Competition; MIT Class of 2009*

The Characteristics of a Good Topic

A good research topic does not simply aim to replicate what has already been established. It does not solely aim to report, but to build upon previous work and pave the way for future explorations. In other words, it must refer to research done in the past and suggest ways of extending the given question in the future. Exemplary research topics often.
• add to a previous model or paradigm;
• challenge a standard model or paradigm;
• clarify or explaining a phenomenon;
• discover something new;
• optimize an existing practice or technique;
• develop a new technique; and/or
• apply knowledge in novel ways.

These characteristics do not necessarily become apparent right away. Through unexpected twists and turns and the discernment of an inquisitive mind, projects can take exciting directions and make seminal contributions to our current scientific knowledge. In sum, great research ideas originate not from a desire to win a science competition, but from a genuine and heartfelt interest to learn, explore and discover.

> "Whatever you do, do something that interests you. It is so much easier to put in the time and energy necessary to do well at these competitions if you are passionate about what you are studying, and your passion (or lack of it) certainly comes across when you write and present your research. Take the initiative to do work that might not necessarily be expected of you. That is what these research programs are

about: using your time to do something extraordinary that no one would expect of a high school student. You will get out of the experience what you put into it. Take advantage of the chance to forge connections with your teachers and other researchers. I am still great friends with my research teachers, and have been able to meet many individuals who I hope to contact as I continue my work on advocating for our nation's veterans. Performing high-quality research as a high school student is a powerful opportunity that I would certainly say is the best thing that happened to me in high school."

Ilana Rice: *Second Place, Young Epidemiology Scholars Competition; Finalist, Junior Science and Humanities Symposium; Semifinalist, Intel Science Talent Search; Barnard Class of 2013*

Take-Home Points

• Successful project ideas take time to develop, so allow ample time for brainstorming.

• All great ideas derive from
  • genuine passion towards the topic;
  • effective background research; and
  • active communication with experts in the field.

• Alertness, curiosity and open-mindedness are crucial for catching serendipitous ideas.

• An exemplary project topic adds something new to an existing field and prompts future investigations.

• Visit the Archimedes Initiative *(www.archimedesinitiative.org)* to see the topical videos, "Choosing Your Experiment" and "Literature Search."

7

Finding a Lab and a Mentor

Every student deserves to be treated as a potential genius.
Anton Ehrenzweig

Introduction

Imagine science as a foreign country that you will be exploring and possibly residing in for the next few years. As an outsider, you are poorly acquainted with the language, laws and customs of this new place, and understandably become overwhelmed and confused by all the novelty. Fortunately, you encounter a hospitable inhabitant who generously takes you to visit the most important regions of this country and offers you temporary lodging while you learn under the benefactor's auspices about the lifestyle and the "ins and outs" of this new land.

Your mentor is the local who familiarizes you with the dynamics of the research world. By introducing you to new scientific knowledge and the way research works, he or she crucially influences your scientific development. It goes without saying that finding a knowledgeable and attentive mentor is one of the first great tasks of your foray into scientific research.

Meeting a Mentor

Not all high school students find mentors by actively searching for scientists with whom to conduct research. Often, students meet their future mentors in activities, programs, competitions and even in classes they attend. Mentors do not necessarily have to be scientists working in laboratories; they can be teachers, judges and even science fair coordinators. Therefore, it is important to keep a constant lookout for potential mentors in the science-oriented part of your life. Meeting mentors during your daily activities, however, is a rare opportunity. Most scientists do not approach high school students and ask them to work on a research project. Rather, students themselves have to take initiative to seek out mentors and persuade these scientists that they are serious about engaging in research. This chapter explains in great detail each step in the process of finding a helpful mentor, and by extension a suitable lab in which you feel comfortable while doing quality research.

> "For high school students, the key to getting the most out of research is to find a strong mentor either in their high school or at a nearby university. In the latter case, be persistent and email the professor frequently. Don't be afraid of not knowing something! You are only a high school student after all. You'll acquire the technical knowledge over time and later in life. At this stage, it's more about learning the process of doing research. Most importantly, have fun! It's thrilling and rewarding to work at the frontier of science."
> **Aman Prasad:** *First Place, Young Epidemiology Scholars Competition; Cornell Class of 2010*

> "I was incredibly fortunate to participate in the Research Science Institute, a summer program held at MIT...I listed some areas that I found interesting and described a couple of problems that I liked and then I was magically matched up with an awesome mentor who guided me along."
> **Benjamin Dozier:** *Finalist, Intel Science Talent Search; Semifinalist, Siemens Competition; Harvard Class of 2012*

> "I met my mentor when I was in middle school, presenting my first astronomy project at the State Science Fair. He was a judge and was impressed with my work. At the end of a long discussion he generously offered to be my mentor for future projects."
> **Philip Mocz:** *Eighth Place, Intel Science Talent Search; Second Place Team, Siemens Competition; Finalist, Intel International Science and Engineering Fair; Finalist, Junior Science and Humanities Symposium; Harvard Class of 2012*

> "What made a huge difference for my project was seeking a mentor at a local university. I would definitely like to encourage high school students to just send emails out! The author(s) of a research article, professor that you read about in a magazine, or someone you find online are all possible candidates to not only help you find a mentor but also to answer questions. Don't be nervous and just have fun with your project! You never know what it could evolve into."
> **Rachel Ginn:** *Fourth Place, sanofi-aventis BioGENEius Challenge; Arizona State University Class of 2012*

The Search

Finding a mentor and finding a lab go hand-in-hand. Usually, students find a lab first by contacting the principal investigator and then meeting the lab researcher who will directly mentor them (whether it is the principal investigator, a post-doc or a graduate student). Regardless of which lab you apply to, finding a lab and a mentor is similar to applying for a job: professionalism and preparation are crucial to success. As in the job market, denials are commonplace but should not be taken personally. You should be ready to contact multiple labs and spend a considerable amount of time familiarizing yourself with their projects, polishing your résumé, and writing cover letters and emails expressing your interest in the research.

Database Perusal

You should have already started your database research while brainstorming project ideas. An efficient way to search for labs of interest is to go to nearby university and institutional websites and find lists of the researchers, their labs and their respective research areas. These websites categorize labs into different research fields, such as immunology, particle physics and synthetic chemistry. Under the fields of your interest, briefly browse through the project descriptions on each lab's webpage and make a list of the labs whose research sounds appealing to you. When determining which labs to contact, keep in mind several important factors that can influence your research experience in that specific environment:

Location

Though seemingly obvious, it is important to find a mentor and laboratory located within a reasonable commute. Factors include the amount of traffic during rush hour, the costs for transportation and the means of transportation. Though most students look for labs whose institutions are located near their homes, usually they have multiple choices of locations. When deciding between labs that are close by and those that are farther away, be sure to take into account the fact that the extra time spent during the commute could be spent doing research. Long commutes, besides taking a significant chunk of your time, can be draining and extremely inconvenient, especially if the lab is nestled amidst urban, high-traffic areas. Distance, however, should not be the main factor influencing your decision, but an issue to consider if you want to eliminate extra headaches that detract from your research experience. Note that this does not apply to summer programs during which you are expected to complete a project in its entirety.

Laboratory Budget

A lab's funding is important to keep in mind because more research money translates into more resources, more freedom of spending and more sustained support of research projects. There is nothing wrong about working in a lab that recycles and reuses basic materials, but a tight budget can keep researchers on a leash and stifle curiosity as they gravitate towards safer, less risky projects. From the students' point of view, less research funding usually means fewer opportunities to explore and experience costly endeavors (i.e., cutting-edge equipment, conferences, etc.). Furthermore, your possible paycheck depends on the lab's ability to support high school student research.

Although finding the exact amount of research grants and monetary awards the lab receives is difficult (if not impossible), a cursory glance at the number of personnel and the number and quality of recent publications can be quite revealing. A greater number of researchers in the lab tends to correlate with higher funding. Similarly, publications in prominent research journals indicate the importance of the work, which is more likely to receive money from funding sources.

Productivity and Quality of Research

Laboratory research often oscillates between more prolific and less prolific periods. Prolificacy, or the number of projects and papers the lab produces each year, usually depends on a seminal discovery or a pivotal idea that spawns many other promising questions to tackle. Some labs operate on a more sluggish pace because the research fields at hand have been over-explored or the ideas have run out of gas. A reliable way to gauge the lab's current prolificacy is to take into account the number of publications in the last two years. The more recent publications the lab has, the more project opportunities it can offer to students. In productive labs, ideas and questions usually float around waiting for someone to address them. High school students are perfect matches for these promising ideological orphans.

Although this should not constitute a significant portion of your search, you can also glimpse the importance of the lab's research by noting the journals in which the research has been published. Publications in well respected journals like *Nature, Science, Cell* and the *Proceedings of the National Academies of Sciences* are usually thought of as pinnacles of scientific achievement. Labs with such renowned journals in their list of selected publications do high-quality research, and can enhance your research experience by exposing you to exemplary science-in-the-making. This is not to say that labs that have not been published on such journals do not conduct stellar research. Be careful not to make the prestige of a lab's publications the overriding factor in your decision. Keep in mind that just because some researchers in the lab engage in world-renowned research does not necessarily mean that they are ready to entrust a high school student with a major project.

Student-Friendliness

Principal investigators differ in their willingness to accept inexperienced students into their labs. Depending on the nature of the research, some labs rarely accept students while other labs welcome research fledglings to explore the science they have to offer. Additionally, mentoring students is not a task any scientist can successfully undertake. Mentoring requires people skills, patience and time. Though it is difficult to tell whether the lab and its personnel are student-friendly until you start working in the lab, the presence of current or past student researchers in the lab is a safe indication that the principal investigator does take students, and that there are scientists in the lab who are experienced in mentoring young scientists.

Reading About a Lab's Research

After you have narrowed your choice to ten or so labs, it is time to do the really important work—familiarizing yourself with the research by reading a selection of their publications. Understanding the lab's research is of paramount importance. In your later email correspondence with the principal investigator, the best way to show you are interested in working in the lab is to convey your knowledge about his or her research. There are certain tips to help you get the most out of your selective reading without spending an inordinate amount of time trudging through scientific jargon. After all, you have to repeat this process for all the labs on your list. Do not ignore the research descriptions on the lab webpage. The descriptions, often written by the principal investigators themselves, summarize their main areas of research. These summaries are good indicators of the layout of the lab's research. Usually, the language in these descriptions is watered down to make the work accessible to the public. Since you need a deeper understanding, pick the publications that interest you most under the selected publications list on the lab website. More often than not, the lab's most important works are showcased in prestigious journals. Read the research published in more widely known journals, as they will most likely include the lab's pivotal research topics.

Reading Scientific Publications for First-time Familiarization

The goal of reading publications during your lab and mentor search is not to become an expert in the field. Instead, your aim is to acquire a general feel of the nature of the lab's research so you can gauge your own interest in that research, write an informed email to the principal investigator and have an informed conversation with him or her in case of an interview.

Select two to four papers to read, preferably one in each area of research. Some lab websites highlight the important papers, and as mentioned, the importance of the work can be indicated by the prominence of the publishing journal.

The first step to reading a scientific paper is to pay close attention to the abstract and the introduction. These two beginning sections provide you with the context and the big picture of the research project, thus aiding your identification of the central question or problem and the motives of the research. In the main body of the paper, take note of the general techniques and approaches used to tackle the problem, but do not focus too much on the specific methodology. The results section tends to be splattered with numbers, acronyms and esoteric names, so do not be bogged down yet by such technicality. Try to understand the figures and tables provided, as they offer a telling visualization of the data and the products of the project. Finally, read the conclusion and discussion sections for a summary of the results. These culminating paragraphs also emphasize the implications and the importance of the project's findings.

After reading each paper, you should have a general idea about the question and problem scientists sought to address, the general approach, the major findings and their implications. Try to brainstorm questions or ideas after reading because these will come in handy when you send an email to the principal investigator.

> "As a high school junior, I wished to spend my summer conducting research in a college laboratory, so I researched the articles published by 12 Princeton and Yale professors, as well as their fields of study. I then contacted each professor to inquire about contributing to his or her laboratory. I spent my summer working at Yale in Professor Margaret Clark's social psychology lab, analyzing the link between personality traits and relationship trends in order to predict marital happiness in participants. The experience taught me the value of taking risks to achieve my objective, as well as helped me to hone my ability to think critically."
> **Chelsea Lynn Jurman:** *Fifth Place, Intel Science Talent Search; Third Place, Young Epidemiology Scholars Competition; Yale Class of 2013*

The Résumé or CV

Selecting labs and reading about their research are part of the grunt work that prepares you to reach out effectively to the principal investigators on your list. There are several components to your efforts of contacting them and persuading them to take you under their supervision. Before writing the all-important email (discussed below), you must have a well organized résumé ready to attach. In addition to your personal email, your résumé is indispensable for making a favorable and professional first impression.

The résumé should portray you as more than just an aspiring researcher or scientist, but as a well-rounded, interesting person worth knowing more about. Pay attention to the organization and layout of the résumé. Although the specific sections can be changed according to your preferences, certain information must be included. These include your contact information (address, email, phone number), your education level, coursework, grades, extracurricular activities (which do not have to be strictly science-related), honors, awards, publications (if applicable), laboratory skills (which should usually be placed at the beginning) and two references (e.g., science teachers or employers) to authenticate your résumé. Be sure to contact your references beforehand to obtain permission to use their contact information. Also, highlight your leadership skills by including the officer positions you have held in student groups, the activities you headed or the projects you started. Although most résumés tend to be one page, there is no harm in slightly exceeding this limit, as long as the extra information about you contributes to your appeal. The following is a general format of an effective résumé:

RÉSUMÉ
Name

CONTACT
Home Address
Email
Phone Number

EDUCATION
High School Name (Years Attended)
Cumulative Unweighted GPA
Selected Coursework and Grades

RESEARCH EXPERIENCE   If Applicable
Position (Dates in this Position)
Laboratory/Institution Name
Supervisor(s)
Brief Description

ACTIVITIES
Activity 1
　　Position (Years Held)
　　Brief Description
Activity 2
　　Position (Years Held)
　　Brief Description
Activity 3
　　Position (Years Held)
　　Brief Description

HONORS AND AWARDS
Award 1 (Year Received)
Award 2 (Year Received)
Award 3 (Year Received)

PUBLICATIONS AND PRESENTATIONS   If Applicable
Publication Names in Correct Bibliography Format

REFERENCES
Reference 1
　　Contact Information
Reference 2
　　Contact Information

The Email

Equipped with an effective cover letter and résumé, you are now ready to write the email to the principal researchers. As the first mode of contact and communication between you and the leading scientist, the email should entice your reader to read your résumé. It should also show that you know about the group's research and display your intense interest in working in the lab. Because some principal researchers may not respond and other labs may be unable to take you, it is important to send emails to a few different labs (at most ten). However, be wary of sending similar emails to multiple researchers in the same department. Though it is understandable for students to send research position applications to several labs, widespread emailing could detract from the genuineness of your appeal in the eyes of some principal investigators.

In your email, introduce yourself as a student eager to engage in science research and who is considering a science research career. Mention that you want to use your project to participate in a science competition. This commitment reveals your seriousness and alludes to your dedication to research. Show the principal investigator that you did your homework by mentioning the publications you have read and the important information you learned after reading the papers. Briefly explain why you chose this lab and why you want to work in the lab. Ask them to refer to your résumé for more details about yourself, your passions and your motivations. If your work will be subsidized by an external source (e.g., high school research grant or summer program), mentioning this will make you more attractive to the principal investigator because it removes the financial strain of paying you.

The email should be written in a formal format with name and greeting on top, followed by the body in block paragraphs and concluded by an appropriate closing phrase. Emails should be a maximum of three paragraphs with no more than five sentences each. In the first paragraph, be sure to introduce yourself and describe the roots of your scientific passion. Why are you interested in science? Why are you interested in the lab's particular field? Avoid generic explanations such as, "I'm fascinated by the mysteries of biology." Be specific. Be concrete. Be creative. Aim for a balance between brevity and detail.

In the next paragraph, describe why you are interested in doing research at that particular lab. This is where you show that you have taken the initiative and read some of the lab's publications. Use phrases like, "I found your recent paper, entitled '....,' very interesting because it demonstrated the novel use of small molecule X. I am interested in helping to elucidate the mechanism of X." If you had any specific questions or ideas that you thought of while reading the paper, feel free to include them in this second paragraph.

In the third paragraph, elaborate on your scientific course load or achievements to show your knowledge or qualifications (do not boast or appear arrogant). Include interesting tidbits about yourself that make you more memorable as a well-rounded human being. While deciding whether to accept you into the lab, principal researchers want to know what kind of person you are. In fact, your character and genuine interest are more important than your scientific accomplishments at this stage. (Since you are a high school student, you are not expected to have cured cancer already.) At the end of the email, do not forget to express your appreciation and thank the reader for his or her consideration of your application. Wait about a week for a reply. If the researcher has not replied after a week, follow up with an email politely inquiring about the receipt of the previous email.

The emails can be reused with modifications for each application to different laboratories. Below is a sample of an effective email:

> Dear [Title Name],
>
> My name is [your name], a [grade level] at [High School Name] and I look forward to doing biomedical research starting this semester. Since my 45-minute introduction to stem cells in my AP Biology class last year, I have been enthralled by the biological versatility of stem cells and their important roles in development, cancer and regenerative biology.
>
> After reading about your current projects and publications regarding the cellular and molecular mechanisms of nuclear reprogramming, I became extremely interested in your research and ask for an opportunity to join the exciting investigations in your lab. The therapeutic and scientific promises of manipulating stem cells deeply fascinate me and your lab's successes in expanding the possibilities of producing stem cell lines [journal citations] intensify my fascination. Certainly, it would be an honor to take part in this cutting-edge research.
>
> My participation in numerous research symposia and science fairs have inspired me to seek a rigorous research experience in a biomedical laboratory. A detailed list of my laboratory skills can be found in the attached CV, which also includes my academic information and other awards. Eventually, I look forward to submitting my work to the Intel Science Talent Search Competition and presenting it at the Intel International Science and Engineering Fair in order to familiarize myself with writing about and communicating science. The experience and knowledge I would gain in your lab would certainly further my ultimate goal of becoming a research scientist who can translate basic research into clinical applications.
>
> Thank you for your consideration,
> [Your name]

It is important to persist in emailing researchers and asking about lab research positions and mentorship. If you do not get a favorable response to any of your first ten emails (which is unlikely), try another ten. Do not be discouraged by denials or lack of responses. Researchers you contact may not be able to take you in as a student researcher because of various reasons, but eventually your hard work will pay off and your email and résumé will attract some offers.

"My sophomore year mentor search was a disaster. I started off emailing and calling professors in enormous batches and ended up with a couple of meetings which pretty much fell apart, despite the potential mentors liking me. In order to stay in my school's program, I had to do a [rather poor quality] summer research program, which served to teach me little more than some computer programming. At the end of that program, I was even more determined to get a mentor in astrophysics, so I went to the nearby Columbia astrophysics department on the pretense of meeting a professor there (he was reluctant to meet when I called, but I persisted). That meeting fell through quickly, so I walked to every door that answered a knock and talked to at least ten professors who were in town, until the last woman I talked to finally seemed interested. Three weeks later she got back to me saying she couldn't take me, but someone she knew—my eventual mentor—could."

Adam Solomon: *Eighth Place, Intel Science Talent Search; Yale Class of 2010*

The Interview

The interview is the principal investigator's way of expressing interest in having you in the lab. He or she wants to meet you and discuss possible projects you can undertake.

For this kind of interview, you should look forward to a relaxed, intellectual and respectful atmosphere. First impressions do matter. Dress nicely in semi-formal clothes, but do not overdress: There is no need for ties, suits, dress pants or formal shoes. You will quickly notice that most researchers are not too concerned about laboratory attire unless a piece of clothing (or lack thereof) poses a serious safety risk.

Prior preparation is essential to a successful and productive interview. Having read some papers before sending out the initial email, you should already know about the lab's research. It is important to go over the research papers again to reengage your memory. (Indeed, it makes a good impression if you have a copy of one or two of the lab's research papers—highlighted—in a folder during the interview.) Be ready to answer general questions about the research and have questions of your own to ask. Your questions will demonstrate your inquisitiveness, a quality that principal researchers look for in students. Finally, it is impressive to bring up ideas, postulates and interesting thoughts during your conversation. Who knows, you might impress the principal researcher with a new insight into the subject. Even if your ideas are not fully formed, your suggestions demonstrate that you are ready to think critically on your own instead of merely following directions from your mentor.

During the interview, sit with good posture and talk with energy and confidence. There is no need to feel nervous. The principal investigator's desire to meet you means that he or she liked your application and wants to get to know you. You probably have more than one foot in the laboratory door already. Never hesitate to ask questions and make sure you talk about the possible project you want to work on. Inquire about the feasibility of finishing the project given the time you will be working in the lab (e.g., during the summer or school year) and even ask about the likelihood of co-authorship on a paper and/or chances of participating in scientific conferences in the future.

Making the Choice That Is Best for You

If you are fortunate enough to receive a few offers from the laboratories you applied to, you must carefully decide which offer to take. It is important that you feel comfortable and satisfied working in the lab you eventually choose. Your attitude towards the lab can impact your performance on your research.

The best way to get a feel of the laboratory environment and personnel is to visit the laboratory and talk to the researchers there. Environments differ from place to place. Some laboratories are smaller but have a more intimate group of researchers. Other laboratories span entire floors and have multiple groups of researchers working on various projects. Decide upon the kind of research milieu that best resonates with you. Also, contact high school or undergraduate students who are currently working or who previously worked in the laboratory and ask them about their experiences—the attention they received from their mentors, the pluses and minuses, the potential of getting published, and certain laboratory idiosyncrasies.

Finally, before you decide to plunge into a lab's research, get to know your mentor if possible. Your mentor is the scientist with whom you will work the closest. As previously mentioned, a good mentor is as important as a good project. Gravitating towards famous, big-name scientists is not always the best approach. They could be too busy with the demands of the scientific community to adequately mentor or interact with a student. An attentive mentor who cares about your scientific growth is more important than a busy luminary trying to maintain and enhance his or her reputation.

Take-Home Points

- Research mentors are not always found in a lab, so be on a look-out in your daily science activities.
- Searching for a suitable lab entails considering its location, budget, research quality, productivity and student-friendliness. All this can be done by perusing laboratory websites and communicating with laboratory personnel.
- In addition to a well-rounded résumé, efficient background reading on a group's research is imperative in writing appealing emails to principal investigators.
- Getting an interview is half the victory; making a great first impression to the principal investigator by showing your enthusiasm and knowledge of his or her research can secure your offer.
- It is important to carefully choose the laboratory based on how its environment and your potential mentor appeal to you.

8

Working in a Laboratory

It is not the strongest of the species that survives, nor the most intelligent, but rather the one most adaptable to change.
Charles Darwin

Introduction

If you are like many other high school students, doing research in a lab will be your first taste of a "real-world" work environment. Lab research will likely be one of your most interesting and overwhelming experiences. In addition to learning copious amounts of new information, you will have to adapt to a new environment governed by unfamiliar rhythms, practices and codes of conduct. It takes time to become comfortable working in a lab, but time is a luxury you cannot afford to misuse. This chapter offers you guidelines to maximize the benefits from your lab experience. It will help you become quickly acclimated to the lab environment so that you do not have to spend too much time orienting yourself; instead you can focus on taking advantage of all the rich opportunities your lab has to offer.

The First Two Weeks—A Rite of Passage

Regardless of which lab you choose to work in and what research field you opt to explore, the steps towards adapting to a new environment and digesting a plethora of information are the same. Students often become disillusioned by the slow pace of the first few weeks and grow impatient while anticipating successful results that often prove elusive. This initial stagnancy is the norm—an unavoidable rite of acclimatization. The key to starting your research experience off on the right foot is to take advantage of the first few weeks by making connections with your lab mates and learning as much as you can. This will help you gain momentum in the days ahead. Below are general experiences you should expect during your first few weeks in the lab. Knowing about them in advance will help you make the most of your laboratory experience.

A Deluge of Information and Background Reading

Mentors usually give their students multiple papers to read during the first few days. The purpose of this is to familiarize new laboratory members with key concepts related to the group's research projects. The purpose of background reading during your first days of work is not merely to obtain a big picture of what you will investigate (something you should already know), but to learn about the nuts and bolts—the technical specifics—of the field so you can use them to devise your own ideas, hypotheses and experiments.

While reading papers, it is important to take your time to digest new knowledge. Do not overwhelm yourself by trying to plow through ten papers in one day. If you are new to reading scientific papers, you might not even finish one paper in a single day. The goal, however, is to absorb and retain the information learned, so do not feel obligated to read as many publications as humanly possible. Take in the new knowledge slowly so that in the near future you can apply it to your own project.

In order to do this, you must read actively and pretend you are analyzing a critical reading passage on the SAT or ACT verbal sections. Search for the main idea, ask questions and summarize paragraphs in your head. After you finish reading each paper, write a brief summary of the main topics and the most important findings so you can internalize most of what you read.

Additionally, ask your mentor and scientists around the lab for anything you do not understand. Do not hesitate to ask questions you think might be obvious. Your fellow lab scientists understand that you are just beginning to delve into the field and will gladly answer any questions you may have.

Days of Monotony: Little to No Work to Do

The first few days will be spent getting situated in the lab. Before starting any experiments, you have to establish your niche in the lab environment. This can entail finding a work desk, setting up a lab email account, getting access to facilities, having medical examinations, learning to operate equipment, taking laboratory safety courses and completing paperwork to register as a research student in the institution. Get these initial chores done immediately so you can start working full-throttle as soon as possible.

Do not expect to perform the main experiments of your research project immediately. Instead, your mentor will show you the proper experimental procedures and lab rules as you follow him or her around throughout the day. The first steps in your lab work can involve ordering reagents, planning the major experiments and doing preliminary experiments to familiarize yourself with a certain protocol.

Do not be fazed or disappointed by an apparent lack of work during the first two or three days. The subsequent workload (and excitement) will often grow exponentially.

Mistakes and Frustrations

The first few weeks are always the hardest: You have to overcome the learning curve consisting of new knowledge and unfamiliar techniques. Mistakes are a normal and integral part of the learning process, especially if you are just beginning to handle something new. Often, your initial experimental results will not be successful. They may be haphazard and inconsistent due to poor technique. Instead of feeling discouraged, consider these initial obstacles as a project in themselves. Think carefully about each step of the experiment and determine what could have gone wrong. Based on your hypotheses, vary your experimental procedures and conditions and check if the results have improved. Troubleshooting is a valuable skill to learn, as it sharpens the investigative skills that are important to solving the theoretical as well as practical problems in your research project.

Awkwardness

Unfamiliarity with the lab mentor and lab personnel can generate stilted conversations, awkward pauses and uncomfortable moments. Do not be held back by awkwardness. The only way to surmount this is to interact with your mentor and other researchers more often. Talk with them whenever you get a chance, not necessarily about science but also about other topics such as politics, pop culture, travel and so forth. An effective way to engage and sustain interesting conversations is to find out the topics each lab member likes to talk about the most. Gravitate towards those topics when you talk with them and you will find yourself in long, interesting conversations that can break the unfamiliarity barrier between you and the other lab members. Making friends with your lab mates is one of the most important things you can do during your time in the laboratory because they will be able to help you when your mentor is unavailable. Also, they can serve as potential recommenders and, in the future, you may work or collaborate with them again. They will most likely be impressed with you already, considering the initiative you took to join the group as a high school student.

Making the Most of Your Lab Experience

Apart from dealing with housekeeping and introductory tasks during the first few weeks, there are other ways you can quickly and comfortably settle into the new lab environment. It is crucial for you to set specific goals for yourself during the first few days in order to avoid a sense of chaos and uncontrollability.

The following two lists consist of measures you can take to make the best of your initial laboratory experience:

Your Project and Project Environment
- Read and understand two or three papers per week.
- Maintain a glossary of all the technical words and terms you encounter.
- Rewrite protocols in your own words. Understand them, ask questions and run through them in your mind.
- Keep an organized binder to archive all the papers you have read and all the experimental protocols you will have to use. (This is important if you want to compete in science fair.)
- Purchase a professional logbook if not provided one. (Chapter 10 details how to keep a logbook.)
- Master at least one technique each week.
- Learn how to operate all the necessary equipment.
- Learn about the locations of all the necessary and important reagents, chemicals, equipment.
- Learn how to order reagents or materials.
- Generate a project timeline with your mentor to stay on top of your experiments and get a sense of how much you can reasonably accomplish given degree of your research commitment and length of your research involvement.
- Learn about the lab's work hours. Can you work alone in the lab during the weekend or do you need supervision? How late can you stay to work?
- Ask about any other lab practices, for example, locking laboratory doors after regular work hours, storing food, discarding waste, answering phones and attending lab meetings.

Your Fellow Researchers and Social Environment
- Learn the names of all of your lab mates.
- Have a rough idea about each person's personalities. Not everyone in the lab may be all smiles and sunshine; you could encounter some inveterate curmudgeons. Do not hold a grudge against them. Learn when and how to interact with them and how not to rub them the wrong way.
- Engage in both scientific and general conversations with your lab mates. Some lab researchers may be more reticent than others and less likely to enjoy personal conversations while others can be very approachable and ebullient, so learn to gauge people's personalities and tailor your interaction with them according to these personalities.
- Learn about protocol (e.g., how should you address and approach your lab PI?).
- Attend as many lab meetings as you can. In addition, actively ask questions and participate in discussions during these meetings.
- Befriend other student interns and research scientists in your lab and the surrounding labs.

Advantageous Long-term Research Habits

After you finally adapt to the new lab environment, there are a few useful practices to maintain in order to ensure sustained success in your research endeavors.

Value Unexpected or Seemingly Wrong Results

Do not offhandedly dismiss results that initially appear to be wrong or contradictory. More than a cursory look is necessary to understand what the data really mean. Depending on the nature of the experiments, many researchers actually spend more time analyzing data than performing experiments. Avoid superficially fixating on the individual data points themselves, but try to connect them, find patterns, relationships, possible explanations and sources of the observed errors. Time and time again, initially unexpected or seemingly wrong results evolve into ground-breaking discoveries.

Learn from the Veteran Researchers

Take advantage of your mentorship and the experts surrounding you by closely observing how your mentor and other researchers conduct research. Look past the cluttered desks and sometimes chaotic lab benches and learn valuable experimental techniques that your mentor does not explicitly tell you. Additionally, pay attention to how scientists around you keep log books and approach problems. Try mimicking their investigative mentality in your own problem solving.

Develop Foresight and Organization

The most effective way of making your experiments run smoothly is to keep yourself organized and plan ahead. Label the materials you use with your name, date and other descriptive information. Store them in a systematic fashion so you can easily find them the next time. Such meticulousness saves precious time and increases your efficiency. Furthermore, before performing each experiment, run through all the steps in your mind and have all the reagents ready and close by. Though experiments can be unpredictable and your research can take drastic turns, you should always plan experiments a week ahead and have a back-up plan in case some experiments do not pan out.

Regularly Update Your Mentor and the Principal Investigator on Your Research Progress

Though it is important to develop independence in your research, keep your mentor and the lab's principal investigator regularly informed about your progress. This way, they can make useful suggestions to your work and you can show them your sustained dedication to the project. Discussing results and ideas with your supervisors also ensures that you all are communicating, which allows you to get to know each other better.

Actively Ask Questions

The habit of asking questions is crucial in the sciences. Questions serve as the fuel that drives the research forward. Broadly speaking, there are two types of questions. The first is more theory based. Examples include: Why does a specific enzyme change its activity in certain conditions or interactions? What contributes to a carbon nanotube's solubility in specific substances? The second deals more with the specific experiments and methods. Examples include: Why is one method used and not the other? What can be done to increase the output or ensure consistency of various trials? These two groups of questions are related to each other and you should consider them in concert. Always try to answer the questions by yourself at first. If they still stump you, ask your mentor and other scientists in the lab.

Good Work Ethic

Good work ethic not only shows your mentor that you are serious about research but also keeps you efficient and organized. Arrive regularly and on time and try to maintain consistent work hours. Your mentor should know when to expect you and should never have to hunt you down or be confused by your irregular schedule. If you cannot make it to lab at a scheduled time, inform your mentor as soon as possible (preferably at least 24 hours in advance).

Be Aware of Intellectual Property Issues

Intellectual property issues in professional research can be very serious, even though they are often overlooked by students who are used to free intellectual property exchange online. Multiple labs often compete against one another to publish results, file patents and find answers to important problems. Always ask your mentor whether you are allowed to divulge your research and research findings in a public setting (e.g., science fairs, school talks). This does not mean that you should refrain from talking about your project to others, but when submitting or exhibiting any part of the data to outside parties, you should always obtain the consent of the lab's principal investigator. Logbooks generally should not leave the lab. Make copies of the pages if necessary, but logbooks are properties of the lab and should be kept within its confines.

Laboratory Safety

Do not take lab safety precautions lightly. Pay attention during safety training session and conscientiously apply what you learn to ensure safe laboratory practices. When in doubt, ask others around you. Never assume that a task is safe if you are not sure about it. Know whom to contact in case of an accident and emergency. Finally, keep emergency contact information close to you, preferably in your cell phone or around your desk and workbench.

Avoid Common Pitfalls

Some high school students become overzealous. Though your research could be one of your top priorities, it should not develop into an obsession at this early stage of your scientific development.

Do Not Become a Lab Hermit

Your lab is not the only research environment in the institution. If time allows, interact with people of other labs. This way, you can develop an overview of the research the institutions supports. While you should delve into your own research area, do not forget to expand your perspective into other areas of science. Doing research in high school is first and foremost a way of helping you decide on your future career aspirations. Do not keep other research options out by locking yourself in your lab. Attend seminars and talks by other researchers. Take advantage of the various resources the institution offers: Visit the scientific library, museums to which you have access and explore other places nearby (not necessarily related to science) that are not easily accessible from your home.

Do Not Become a Lab Rat

Though a few graduate students and post-doctoral fellows do at times camp out in the lab, regularly working from early morning to late at night (and even working overnight) is neither healthy nor productive. Incessant lab work wears scientists out. It is imperative that you take breaks and perform your experiments with a fresh mind. The most successful researchers are those who can strike a balance between research and personal life. Find ways of maximizing your work efficiency so that you have time to enjoy other aspects of the work environment and of your life.

Culminating Your Research Experience

Regardless of whether you are participating in a science fair, compiling your work and presenting your results to other students and scientists at the end of your research experience should be one of your end goals. Summer research programs often have symposia and project presentation assemblies for students to showcase their posters or slide presentations summarizing their projects. If you are not involved in a research program, you should still present your project during a lab meeting. Your project does not have to be at all complete at the end of your research experience. In fact, your research is almost expected to be incomplete given the time constraints and your level of experience. The goal of presenting your work to other scientists is not only to show them your work and knowledge, but also to obtain more formal feedback on your research. Other scientists may voice insightful comments, suggestions and views that can facilitate your own understanding of the project, suggest ways to improve it and provide future problems you can tackle. Most importantly, synthesizing all the knowledge and data you have gathered in the lab is a wonderful practice for communicating science—a skill that is paramount in research and in your development as a potential research scientist.

Successful research experiences result when you take initiative to absorb the science and the work environment around you. Ultimately, it is up to you to determine whether your laboratory experience will be a positive one. You are offered a valuable opportunity to explore the exciting mysteries of science. Use this opportunity well.

Take-Home Points

• The first few days in a lab can present many challenges, such as information overload, initial monotony, frustration with experiments and awkwardness with lab personnel, all of which can be quickly overcome by following simple guidelines regarding efficient research practices and social interactions within the lab.

• After initial acclimatization, there are a few long-term research habits like foresight, good work ethics and keen observation you can adopt to maximize the success of your project and scientific development.

• Avoid being obsessed with your own research; expand your scientific perspective by exploring and learning from your entire scientific and social surroundings.

• Culminate your research experience by presenting your work to your lab mates and student peers.

9

Impressing Your Mentor

It is not worth impressing one's professor simply for the sake of impressing one's professor—such superficial posturing can only come across as what it truly is. Rather, I would recommend that you just try your best and allow the true genius beneath the surface peek through, like a shaft of sunlight through the clouds.

Greg Brockman: *Sixth Place, Intel Science Talent Search; Semifinalist, Siemens Competition; Finalist, Junior Science and Humanities Symposium; MIT Class of 2012*

Introduction

Mentors have a personal stake in your success. Your achievements under their supervision often reflect on their ability to successfully nurture a potential member of the next generation of researchers. Even if your mentor does not think so altruistically or far into the future, your success can be an asset to his or her résumé, credentials and reputation. Impressing your mentor should certainly not be an end in itself. Instead, your goal should be to work hard toward a fruitful research experience. While striving toward this goal, you will automatically impress your mentor with your genuine dedication to the group's research. Therefore, a great way of impressing your mentor is taking steps to ensure your own success in research. Following the advice that this chapter provides will certainly help you impress your mentor and everyone else in the lab. Most importantly, this advice will keep you secured on the track to research success.

The Student-Mentor Relationship

To better understand why and how to impress your mentor, you must have a clear grasp of the nature of a student-mentor relationship. While the student and the mentor do interact on friendly terms, the mentor cannot accurately be described as a "friend" in the sense of a confidant or comrade. A mentor is a guide—a person with extensive knowledge and experience in a field who oversees and assists the student's development in research. An exemplary mentor keeps a healthy distance from the student: He or she gives the student certain pointers, but allows the student to develop independence and self-reliance in research.

At the same time, your relationship with your mentor should not entirely resemble a boss-employee relationship. Far from assuming a hierarchical give-and-take power dynamic, the student-mentor relationship takes on a more collaborative atmosphere. Students must go beyond passively absorbing information. They should ingest and synthesize knowledge and never be afraid of (respectfully) questioning the mentor's instruction. Because of its interactive nature, such a relationship requires that both the student and the mentor do their parts in adhering to certain guidelines and rules of conduct.

The Student's Responsibilities

Although you are encouraged to voice your opinions and suggestions (even if they conflict with your mentor's propositions), you should always respect your mentor since he or she is a more experienced scientist. Not everything they do or espouse may be correct. After all, veteran scientists are still human beings prone to making mistakes. However, you should always take your mentor's words seriously and behave cordially in your mentor's presence.

Additionally, do not expect too much from your mentor in terms of dedicating time to guide you. You must acknowledge that your mentor has research obligations of his or her own and cannot serve as a research babysitter. In addition, your mentor may have many advisees ranging from high school students like yourself to post-doctoral researchers. Therefore, do not feel disappointed or slighted if your mentor cannot attend to your needs all the time. Just as acclimating to a lab environment is a challenge for you, so is balancing mentorship and research responsibilities a challenge to your mentor.

Finally, report any issue involving your project to your mentor first. Since your mentor is in charge of you and your research, he or she should be the first person to contact in matters involving your laboratory work. This includes, but is not limited to, experimental difficulties, sharing results with people outside your lab and testing a new idea. Situations jeopardizing your safety and health could be a rare exception. In these cases, contact and report immediately to the health office if necessary and ensure your well-being first before informing your mentor.

The Mentor's Responsibilities

Despite having more experience and knowledge, the mentor should not patronize the student and belittle the student's theoretical and experimental contributions to research. The mentor should similarly respect the student as a growing scientist.

Mentoring a high school student is a serious commitment, so the mentor should conscientiously guide the student and answer questions. The mentor should never focus on his or her own research to the point of abandoning the student to the vagaries of science. A mentor's job is to provide advice, insight and constructive criticism about the project and research in general. In doing so, the mentor should regularly check on the student (asking for result reports, overseeing experiments, etc.) to make sure the student stays on the right path.

Why Impress Your Mentor?

Your mentor will mold your research experience and influence your future aspirations. Therefore, you have a significant portion of your success invested in your mentor's impression of you as a young researcher. A sufficiently impressed mentor will be invaluable to your present and future undertakings, from college applications to your development as a scientist.

College Recommendations

College admission officers look favorably on positive recommendations from people outside of your high school who have personally and professionally interacted with you. Every applicant is going to have teacher and counselor recommendations, but not everyone can supply a recommendation from a research scientist. Your mentor's comments on your scientific development, lab work and research skills can provide additional, favorable insights into your character—a supplement that can give you an edge over the other applicants.

Future Job References

The relationships and connections you develop in high school research can last even beyond college. In your future job searches, your mentor can serve as a reliable and impressive reference to vouch for your work ethic and other appealing qualities. Endorsements from established scientists who can attest to your ability to excel in a laboratory environment can be extremely advantageous, especially if you apply to the same or a similar research institution.

Your Mentor's Dedication to You

The student-mentor relationship is a positive feedback loop that hinges upon your ability to prove to your mentor your dedication to research. A mentor who holds you in high regard tends to give you more attention and conscientious guidance. In short, your commitment to your work translates into your mentor's commitment to your scientific growth. Nurturing mentors will help you become more enthusiastic about research, thus increasing your involvement in laboratory work.

Your Overall Learning Process

Impressed mentors show more respect towards their students. As a result, mentors may treat their mentees more like collaborators than apprentices. This higher level of esteem encourages more sophisticated and meaningful exchanges through which mentors can share insights into a research topic that they would not normally share with a high school student. Furthermore, mentors can provide more opportunities (e.g., allowing the student to present research at meetings and symposia) to the students who they think have achieved a high level of proficiency in a field.

Impressing Your Mentor on All Fronts

Impressing your mentor is neither a sporadic nor temporary effort. Rather, because your mentor's opinion of you substantiates (and possibly changes) as time passes, it is important to continuously strive for the best impression. As mentioned before, the driving force for your behavior should not be to impress your mentor, but to make the most of your research experience. Impressing your mentor requires that you demonstrate not only hard work and intellect, but also a commendable character. There are several components to your self-presentation, which when improved will enhance both your image and your overall research experience.

Speech

Speech is the main and the most obvious line of communication linking you to your mentor. Therefore, it is essential to pay attention to not only what you say, but also how you say it. Overly self-conscious students often feel nervous when talking to their scientific superiors in fear of presenting themselves in the wrong way. Anxiety, however, can only detract from the quality of the verbal exchange. When talking to your mentor, relax. Make a conscious effort to speak confidently, audibly and slowly. Speaking slowly will allow you to think before vocalizing each sentence, thus facilitating more articulate responses and conversations.

Writing

Though writing to your mentor is limited to emails, letters and reports, showing your mentor that you have effective writing skills can serve as a plus. While composing emails, be careful of how you address your mentor. Some mentors ask the students to address them by their first names only (this applies also in conversations), but others ask for more formal titles. Regardless of their preference, do not be too informal in emails and letters. Also, pay close attention to grammar, syntax and spelling, as egregious slips in those departments can hurt your mentor's impression of you.

> "...it's also helped that I can communicate and collaborate effectively with my mentor and other researchers, both informally and through emails (especially important when your mentor is away a lot) and formally through my articles and grant proposals."
> **Philip V. Streich:** Intel Foundation Young Scientist, Intel International Science and Engineering Fair; Third Place, Intel Science Talent Search; Regional Finalist, Siemens Competition; Davidson Fellow Laureate; United States Physics Olympiad Team; Harvard Class of 2013

Discipline

Always maintain good work habits. Be punctual to work and lab meetings, and do your best to obey deadlines. In extenuating circumstances, notify your mentor ahead of time. Additionally, keep an organized workspace, with clean and tidy desks, notebooks and logbooks.

Personality and Individuality

Remember that to your mentor, you are not merely an automaton destined for scientific grooming. You are an individual, a person possessing endearing qualities that separate you from others. Show your mentor that you have character, that you are an interesting human being. Let your mentor know about your fascinating background, your upbringing, your dreams and your funny stories. Even if you do not have colorful tidbits to share about your life, strive to be energetic, honest, generous and understanding toward all the other lab members. Be friendly and helpful to other laboratory members. Socialize and get to know them and open your mind to all the different kinds of scientists in the laboratory group.

Professionalism and Quality of Research

Professionalism and effective research skills are the qualities most relevant to your mentor. Above all, your mentor wants to gauge your scientific development under his guidance. The more you improve and the faster you refine your research skills, the more satisfied your mentor will be. Have high standards for your work and constantly strive for the high quality of projects showcased in peer-reviewed scientific journals. Be rigorous about conducting controlled experiments, analyzing data and writing reports, and be professional when presenting them to your mentor, your lab and the public.

Initiative

Along with professionalism and quality of research, your initiative is very appealing to your mentor because it reflects your active engagement and independence in research. Take full ownership of your project by asking questions, suggesting new ideas, approaches and explanations. Volunteer to present your data at lab meetings. Be observant and take initiative to clean and organize the lab environment when necessary.

> "I impressed my mentor with my interest and enthusiasm in the research. I was not afraid to discuss my ideas with her and she encouraged me to continue my independent thinking. It may be important to impress the professors you work with because they enjoy learning ideas from the students as much as the students enjoy learning from them."
> **Xiaoli Mi:** *Finalist, Intel International Science and Engineering Fair; Harvard Class of 2012*

Productivity

A surefire way to impress your mentor is to generate good data in short periods of time. Do not dawdle on the Internet (e.g., Facebook and emails). Whenever you have free time, optimize efficiency by planning future experiments, analyzing past data and reading relevant publications. There are always ways to broaden your research experience. You merely have to put your mind to it.

Making Your Hard Work More Apparent

Sometimes, being diligent in the lab is not enough to impress a mentor. Some mentors are so busy that you have limited opportunities to interact with them each day. In such cases, it is important to take advantage of the valuable times when you have your mentor's attention and maximize how often he or she witnesses your research efforts. You can be the hardest working individual in the lab, but without actively making your mentor aware of your dedication, your efforts will slip by unappreciated.

Be Smart with Your Work Schedule

Whenever possible, coordinate your work schedule with your mentor's work schedule. If your mentor arrives early for work, follow his or her lead and try your best to come to the laboratory early. On the other hand, if your mentor is one of those scientists who usually stays late in the lab, do try to stay late as often as you can. This is not to say that you should adopt the ten-hour plus workday schedule that some research scientists religiously follow, but be around as much as possible when your mentor is around so that he or she is aware of your constant presence and hard work. After your mentor goes off work, avoid staying in the lab unless absolutely necessary. For one, your mentor is not present to witness your hard work. More importantly, your mentor will not be around to help you if you encounter specific problems with your experiments. Overall, be smart with your work schedule, but do not fixate upon it. Having concrete results to show your mentor will impress him or her more than just sticking around in the lab.

Show Your Mentor All Your Grunt Work

Results illustrate only one part of your arduous research journey. All your thoughts, planning, calculations and scribbles leading up to the data are important components of your work that must be displayed to your mentor. Do not show your mentor only the end product of your tasks; let your grunt work reveal the ongoing effort of arriving at the results. The process of answering a question is just as remarkable as the answer itself. Therefore, do not let your labor go unappreciated. Give your mentor quick updates and reports on your investigative process, on the results and on the future directions of your research. In addition to impressing your mentor with your rigorous involvement in the project, such regular updates will keep your mentor more involved as well.

Asking for a Letter of Recommendation

One of the main benefits of impressing your mentor is obtaining an impressive letter of recommendation at the end. After weeks or even months of dedication to research, it is finally time to reap the fruits of your hard work. Asking for a letter of recommendation sometimes requires certain preparation and a plan of action.

The most important preparation is foresight. Give your mentor ample time—more than two weeks—to write a recommendation letter. Research scientists have demanding schedules. Many of them race against time to publish results and finish projects. In addition, research conferences and meetings can keep them quite busy. Since a thoughtful recommendation takes time to write, you must allow your mentor enough time to fit your request into his or her schedule. Due to the amount of work researchers have, it is not uncommon for mentors to forget your recommendation in the midst of their research pandemonium, so gentle weekly reminders help ensure that your request is always on their to-do list.

As is usual for recommendation requests, provide your mentor with a comprehensive résumé. However, be sure that your mentor does not just restate the accomplishments presented on your résumé; rather, he or she should offer fresh insights into your abilities not included in your résumé and on high school teacher recommendations. Furthermore, accounts of personal interactions and anecdotal details make the recommendation many times more appealing to the reader. There is no harm in stressing these points to your mentor. In fact, politely offering recommendation guidelines facilitates your mentor's task.

Finally, provide your mentor with an envelope in which to enclose your recommendation and thank him or her (with a card and, when appropriate, a small gift) for his or her guidance throughout your research journey. In some cases, your mentor might even invite you back to extend the work you have already so diligently accomplished in the lab.

To learn more about the importance and qualities of exemplary student-mentor relationships, read a feature article in *Nature* available (for free access) online: Lee, A., Dennis, C. and Campbell, P. *Nature*'s guide for mentors. *Nature* 447, 791-797 (2007).

Take-Home Points

• Impressing your mentor should not be an end in itself; your mentor will naturally be impressed with the effort you invest in research productivity, work discipline, self-presentation and personal growth.
• Impressed mentors can serve as invaluable assets to your college applications, future job applications and your scientific development.
• Visit the Archimedes Initiative *(www.archimedesinitiative.org)* to see the topical video, "Mentors."

- To learn more about the importance and qualities of exemplary student-mentor relationships, read a feature article in *Nature* available (for free access) online: Lee, A., Dennis, C. and Campbell, P. *Nature*'s guide for mentors. *Nature* 447, 791-797 (2007).

10

The Importance of Keeping a Logbook

Writing is like driving a car at night. You never see further than your headlights, but you can make the whole trip that way.
E. L. Doctorow

On the most basic level, a logbook is a journal in which you record every step of your experiment as you conduct it: your lab notebook is the official record of what you did; however, any experienced laboratory researcher will tell you that a logbook has so much more to offer. Your logbook is a good place to brainstorm ideas and to record questions as they crop up as well as the answers when you find them. Accurate recordkeeping can be a huge asset to you as you conduct research, to your mentor and colleagues long after you have moved on from the lab and to your performance in competitions. Preparing your logbook will also be useful practice for the many laboratory classes that you will take in college, should you continue studying science.

Ideally, your logbook will be written in pen and organized by date, containing an entry for each time you worked on your research project. It is surprising how quickly you may forget aspects of your experiment if you do not write them down. Standard practice dictates that you should never rip out any pages from the notebooks, nor leave blank pages. Any errors should be crossed out with a single line (never white them out). If you have typed up step-by-step protocols it is a good idea to paste the print-out in the notebook for future reference. Creating spreadsheet templates which automatically perform calculations for you can be useful. These can be easily printed out for your logbook and modified when necessary. Also, for the purpose of science competitions, it is often a good idea to include photographs in your lab notebook of equipment used and of any visual results. If you have many images, such as microscopy images, you may want to include these in a separate three-ring binder as a supplement to your logbook; however, it is important that everything be accurately labeled and dated.

In addition to explaining exactly what you did, you should also use your logbook to catalog practical information for future reference, such as detailed specifications of your experimental materials. For example, when you use a particular antibody or chemical solution, it is often a good idea to tape the product insert right into your lab notebook. This method saves you time and assures that you will have all the important facts about the product accurately recorded. A piece of information you may not expect to be useful could turn out to be critical later on. For example, if you have been getting great results with an antibody from a particular company and a particular lot number, you will want order more from the same lot. Likewise, if your experiments start to fail you may need to look back to earlier steps that you have recorded in your logbook to figure out what went wrong. Since you will know what you have tried already, you can use this to make adjustments and refine your techniques. Your lab notebook will help you to communicate precisely about the situation with your mentor. Diligent record keeping will assure your mentor that you are confident in the work you have done. If you cannot confidently tell your mentor how you performed a particular procedure, and that procedure failed, he or she will almost certainly ask you to repeat the task. Thus, in all of these situations, and countless others, the time and effort you invest in keeping accurate records will save you substantial time and effort in the future.

Alexis Mychajliw, who conducted ecology field research, created her own fieldwork note sheets to be used in collecting the specific data points she needed. Alexis caught hundreds of dragonflies and damselflies and kept records of where they lived, what behavior they were performing and what species and gender they were. For Alexis' research, accurate and detailed records were especially important, because slight variation in environmental conditions were likely to skew her results and conclusions: "It was exceedingly important for me to keep accurate records of every field outing, including menial things such as temperature and weather conditions, because since I was working in an actual environment, I could not take any one variable for granted... my entire thesis was based upon the movement and response of a certain fragment of the total sample size." Whether you realize it or not, the details matter and you should record any irregularities that occur as you conduct your experiments. These may become important in understanding your results later.

If you are not yet impressed by the many benefits your logbook can offer you, consider what the logbook means to your mentor. He or she has been generous enough to share his or her time, expertise and research grant dollars with you. In exchange, it is only courteous to make sure that at the end of your time in the lab your mentor has written record of what you did. Your mentor will expect you to document your work thoroughly and will appreciate the effort you put into your lab notebook. Do not frustrate or disappoint your mentor with shoddy notes! A few years down the road, another person in your lab may need to use your logbook to try to reproduce your results. Carefully documenting what you have done will also work to your advantage if you plan on trying to get your research published.

Dayan Li, who won top honors at the Intel International Science and Engineering Fair (ISEF) can attest to the critical importance of the logbook. He notes that while papers and other publications are forms in which you *communicate* your research, the logbook is your actual *"immortalized research."* As Dayan points out, the logbook is a critical supporting document to your poster display, because it documents every step of your journey and should contain every detail of your work. While your poster presents the work as a whole, the logbook is an important indicator of how independently you worked. You should state clearly in your logbook which parts of your project you did and also acknowledge which parts you were helped with. Science fair judges, who are scientists themselves, will be interested in seeing how thoroughly you documented your work since this allows others to reproduce it in the future.

For many reasons, diligent recordkeeping in your logbook is an essential part of your ability to conduct successful laboratory research. The time you invest creating the logbook will pay for itself many times over. Not only will you make life easier for yourself by keeping accurate notes, you will also seize an important and relatively easy opportunity to impress your mentor and others evaluating your research, such as competition judges. By putting together an excellent logbook, you will also guarantee that your research is preserved in its most original, authentic form for future reference by yourself and others.

Take-Home Points

- Keeping a thorough record of your research is valuable for you, for your research and for your mentor.
- Documenting your work will allow you to make sure that you understand what you are doing as you conduct research and that you remember what you did months ago. Keeping a logbook takes time, but it is critical for interpretation of results, troubleshooting and for others to replicate your work. Good scientific practice dictates that your research should be able to be independently replicated by others.
- A logbook is also critical for your mentor after you have left the lab and may help your contributions to be recognized if your data is published in the future.

Part III:
Elements of a Successful
Research Project

11

Using the Scientific Method to Your Advantage

An education isn't how much you have committed to memory, or even how much you know. It's being able to differentiate between what you know and what you don't.
Anatole France

The scientific method is a framework you can use to guide your experimental research. Briefly, the scientific method consists of asking a research question, developing an informed hypothesis or prediction about its answer, and then designing an experiment to test that hypothesis. It is essential that a researcher clearly establish his or her research question and hypothesis, in order to conduct an experiment with interpretable, meaningful results. Upon obtaining results, one then uses the scientific method again to ask a follow-up question. As the process repeats over and over again, researchers working independently can build upon each other's work to add to the general knowledge of a field. The scientific method provides a guide for what to do when one does not know what one is doing. It is a sort of a code that all scientists follow in order to conduct quality research and is used to understand and evaluate the research of others. In addition to providing guidelines for how to develop and conduct your experiment, this chapter will discuss appropriate and ethical interpretation of data.

Research Question

Determining what question you want to answer through your research is the first and arguably the most important step of the scientific method. Select an important, novel research question, one that is answerable using experimental techniques available to you. It is also important that you seek to evaluate something that is measurable, either through quantitative or qualitative means. You should think carefully about what type of results you hope to get out of your experiment as you are planning it out—for example, whether you should use quantitative or qualitative analysis methods is discussed later in this chapter. Regardless of whether you plan to enter your research in a competition, you should consider how your fellow researchers and experienced scientists (possibly judges) would view your experimental design and the results it will produce. Does your experimental design actually address the question you hope to answer—or are you unwittingly addressing more than one question at once? Would there be a more direct way to test the same question?

Hypothesis

A hypothesis is an informed prediction about the answer to your research question. You may base your hypothesis on previous observations made by yourself or others. Thus, it is important to conduct background research so that you are well-versed on what is known about your research topic. The National Center for Biotechnology Information's (NCBI) PubMed is an excellent resource for those researching in the biological sciences to find out what has been published on their topic in the past. It is important to make sure that your research question is novel—it has not been previously answered. Reading current papers in the field will allow you to understand how your work fits in to the body of research that has been done in the field. It is a good exercise to write a research paper to summarize what you have learned through background reading. This paper will be useful in preparing displays and paper submissions for competitions later.

Experimental Design Primer

Once you have a good grasp of your research field and have delineated your research question and hypothesis, the next step is to design an experiment to test your hypothesis. Fundamental principles of experimental design are discussed here. In designing your experiments, you should take into account personal and environmental safety, as well as rules that apply to research-based competitions. For example, many competitions require that your research plan be approved by an Institutional Review Board (IRB) beforehand, to make sure that it is safe. Regardless of whether you plan to enter competitions, there are certain safety considerations everyone should take into account when designing and conducting research. Before starting any experimentation, you should consult the rules of major research competitions, such as the Intel Science Talent Search, Intel International Science and Engineering Fair and Siemens Competition for Math, Science and Technology.

Many experiments are designed to test the effect of an *independent variable* on a *dependent variable*. For example, you might set out to determine the effect of temperature on plant growth. If there is indeed a relationship between these two variables, then temperature would be the independent variable, and plant growth would be the dependent variable, since its value depends on the temperature. All other independent values that might affect plant growth should be held constant. To test this hypothesis, one could grow several plants of the same type under various temperature conditions. All plants would otherwise be treated exactly the same, given the same amount of water, soil, fertilizer and light.

Controls are components of an experimental design that can be used to rule out alternative explanations of results. Controls may be *positive* or *negative*. Positive controls are set up in such a way that they should deliver a positive result, based on previous experience. Similarly, negative controls are set up in such a way that they should deliver a negative result. Negative controls can also be used to provide a baseline or background value that can be compared to (and in some cases subtracted from) experimental results values. A simple example of how to use positive and negative controls is explained below; however, remember that in more complex experimental settings the importance of controls increases tremendously! It is hard to overemphasize the importance of controls—you will want to be absolutely sure that you conducted the correct controls so that you can interpret your results accurately.

Suppose that you wanted to test the efficacy of three concentrations of bleach (diluted in water) in preventing mold growth. Based on previous experience, you are certain that if you leave a piece of bread to sit out for two weeks, mold will grow on it.

In addition to having three slices of bread treated with three bleach solutions, you must have a fourth piece of bread treated with water alone as a *positive control*. In this way you will accomplish several things: 1) you will ascertain your expectation that mold grows on bread in the period of time and under the conditions you are using, 2) you will assess how much mold grows without bleach treatment, which you may want to use as a basis for comparison when you evaluate the efficacy of each bleach dilution. You would be surprised if no mold grew on the positive control slice of bread. If your positive control gave an unexpected negative result (no mold grew on the control slice of bread), then you would know that something about the experimental setup was flawed.

Because good controls are critical to good research, you may want to consult an experienced scientist to make sure you have planned out the appropriate controls. They will be able to check your reasoning, and it is likely that they will suggest additional factors for which you should set up controls. For the purposes of entering scientific competitions, you should be completely clear on why you chose to do particular controls and not others. Judges are (rightfully) very interested in making sure you understand the concept of controls for yourself, even if you had help designing your controls.

Gathering Results

Your research question may lend itself to quantitative analysis, or you might need to rely on qualitative observations because of technical limitations.

Quantitative analysis, which uses numerical measurements, is generally preferable to non-quantitative analysis, because it allows for statistical analysis. Applying statistical analysis to your data allows you to examine whether your results could have occurred due to random chance. Qualitative data is, of course, also acceptable; however, most qualitative results may be made stronger through incorporation of quantitative tools. Suppose one wanted to determine which of ten chemical solutions is most corrosive. One way would be to apply each solution to a separate piece of metal and to evaluate each sample by sight, describing the relative corrosiveness of the solutions. Alternatively, in addition to your descriptive observations, you could use a number as a surrogate for your description. When your results are open to human error or subjective interpretation, it is also a good idea to incorporate blinding into your results interpretation. In the example above, you could "blind" the name of each solution by having another person identify each solution with a number, and keeping that list private. The important concept of blinding is that the identity of each solution remains unknown to the individual evaluating the results, so that it does not, consciously or unconsciously, bias their interpretations. It is important that you repeat your experiments multiple times in order to demonstrate that you can replicate your results. This will make your findings more believable to yourself and others. Never trust a result that you got only once. Also, you should never discount or misrepresent a result because it was not what you expected to see. As Wendy Zhang rightly pointed out, "Fraud in scientific research is a crime. You cannot manipulate your data to get the results you want. Nature is nature, it cannot be changed. Any findings you discover are important, whether positive or negative."

Results Analysis

Once you have obtained your results, you must evaluate whether your hypothesis is valid, invalid or whether you cannot determine the validity of your hypothesis. Basic statistical analysis is a must if you have collected quantitative data, because this will allow you to ascertain that your results did not occur due to chance. For example, if you were measuring the heights of 100 men and 100 women in order to ask whether men or women are generally taller, you would compare the average heights between groups. Perhaps the average height of your sample male population was only slightly greater than that of the sample female population. You will want to know whether this is a "real" difference or whether this difference occurred by chance. This could happen as a result of the individuals you selected to participate in your experiment. Consult publications in your field in order to determine the appropriate statistical tests you will need. Frequently, the Student's t-test is appropriate for determining whether quantitative differences between two groups are statistically significant. This basic form of statistical analysis allows the researcher to determine the validity of the "null hypothesis," which states that there is not a difference in a measurement between two groups. The t-test allows one to calculate the probability that a quantitative difference between groups occurred due to chance, and to express this probability as a p-value. Generally, when a p-value is below 0.05 or 5%, one can reject the "null hypothesis" and conclude that there is a "statistically significant" difference between two groups; however, this does not mean that a difference is real, or important. Remember, it is generally better to make a tentative conclusion rather than an overreaching one.

Ideally, if your question, hypothesis and experimental design were perfectly mapped out, you would be able to judge your hypothesis as valid or invalid; however, in real life research is not always so clear-cut. Perhaps your results were difficult or impossible to interpret, or perhaps something completely unexpected happened that forces you to reconsider your experimental design. If this happens to you, do not despair—many great discoveries have been made just this way. Thoughtful evaluation of what happened with your experiment is very valuable, regardless of whether your initial hypothesis was valid. If your hypothesis was incorrect, the scientific method dictates that you should formulate a new hypothesis based on what you have learned. Then you design a new experiment and the process repeats itself. This is how scientists conduct real-world research: through well-planned iterations of the scientific method. Regardless of whether you plan to carry out further experimentation, you should think about alternative hypotheses to explain your results and how you could test those experimentally. If you plan to enter scientific competitions, it is always a good idea to have thought about the implications of your experiment for further research, because judges may want to discuss this with you.

Communicating Your Results

The final step of the scientific method is to communicate your results. If you have done your "homework" in the initial stages of the scientific method, you will already have a clear understanding of what you set out to do and how you conducted your research. Sharing this information with others will be relatively straightforward provided that you have put in the necessary thought and effort in the initial planning stages. Create clear, well-labeled graphs of your most important results. Resist the temptation to create a multitude of graphs when you could more succinctly and effectively convey your results with one or two well-thought-out graphs. For the purposes of competition and presentation, displaying too much information devalues the important graphs and overwhelms the viewer with unimportant data. You will want to prepare an abstract which concisely summarizes your project (a good target length is 250 words). The abstract should introduce and provide rationale for the research question, as well as discuss the hypothesis, experimental setup and the most important results and their significance to the field.

Take-Home Points

- The scientific method is a tried and true guide for conducting research.
- Constantly ask yourself, "What is my research question?" Having a good research question which can be fairly tested by your experimental methods is absolutely essential.
- "The data are the data." Experiments do not always work and they frequently do not tell you what you expected them to. "Listen" to your data and make sure that you do not over-interpret your data. Be transparent and say only what you can fairly say. A mature scientist has the integrity to acknowledge the limitations and potential caveats of his or her experiments.
- Become a part of a scientific community; science is more fun when you engage with your colleagues and experts in your field. Communicating your research and learning about the research of others are important parts of the scientific method.
- Visit the Archimedes Initiative *(www.archimedesinitiative.org)* to see the topical video, "Designing Your Experiment."

12

Writing a Publishable Research Paper

Language is the only instrument of science....
Samuel Johnson

Publication of research is a critical validation, both of the research work and of the author. Indeed, there are few experiences as fulfilling as publishing a research paper in a respectable, peer-reviewed journal.

Although students often believe that publication is out of reach, many top students—even high school students—have published their research results. Publication is possible, but requires early commitment and continued focus, as well as close planning and interaction with the research mentor.

This chapter details the elements of a publishable research paper, remarking on the differences between the "publication" draft—which is submitted to a journal—and the "science fair" draft—which a student submits to science fairs. This chapter then discusses the steps of the publication process.

The discussion in this chapter will presume some familiarity with the format of scientific research papers, hence a reader unfamiliar with scientific papers should be sure to examine examples while perusing this chapter.

Content

Nearly all professional research papers are grown about the same skeleton of sections: abstract, introduction, "guts" (which includes all the novel scientific content of the paper), conclusion, references and attribution. Each of these sections will be addressed in turn. The content of science fair papers is similar to that of publication-format papers, hence this subsection may also be read in preparation for composing the science fair draft.

It should be noted that these instructions are guidelines, rather than rules. Many journals or conferences have special content or formatting requirements. Specific instructions from publication venues (or the research mentor!) should always supersede the suggestions of this *Guide*.

> "Regarding how to write [the paper], ask your adviser! Different fields have different requirements. Always keep in mind, however, that scientific writing is different from everyday prose."
> **Greg Brockman:** *Sixth Place, Intel Science Talent Search; Semifinalist, Siemens Competition; Finalist, Junior Science and Humanities Symposium; MIT Class of 2012*

Abstract

Every scientific paper should open with a brief abstract which summarizes the key results and methods of the work. The abstract should excite and impress, as many readers will read no further.

Although the abstract is the first section any reader will read, it should be the last section the author writes. Thus, it will be addressed at the end of this subsection.

Introduction

The introduction is one of the most important sections of the research paper. A good introduction should define relevant technical terminology, place the research work in context, indicate the work's importance and lay out the structure of the paper. While this discussion should be concise, it must be thorough.

Professional academic papers are not essays. They rarely open with allusive quotes or broad statements. The introduction should cut straight into the material; language indicating the relevant research field and subfield should appear in the very first sentences. (See the example of a first introductory paragraph, given below.)

It is essential that all technical terms be defined the first time they appear. Such terms should also be italicized or otherwise highlighted, to draw the reader's focus. Conversely, most relevant technical terminology should appear—and hence be defined in—the introduction.

Amidst the definitions, the introduction should contain a survey of the literature on the research topic. This survey should place the research work in context and should indicate the author's command of the literature. (These dual purposes of the literature review are especially important to both referees and science fair judges.)

The last paragraph of the introduction should be a "road map" of the paper. This paragraph, which functions like an extended abstract, should be written late in the drafting stage. It should indicate the contents of later sections of the paper. Most importantly, all the research results should be summarized in this paragraph. (See the example of a final introductory paragraph, given below.)

Annotated Example of a First Introductory Paragraph

from Adam R. Solomon's "The Effects of Age on Brown Dwarf Spectral Features in the Near-Infrared": *Third Place, Siemens Competition; Eighth Place, Intel Science Talent Search; Yale Class of 2010*

> [1] The past decade has seen a rebirth in the field of stellar astronomy with the discovery of a unique class of celestial objects called brown dwarfs. [2] Brown dwarfs are "failed stars," objects forming in the same way as typical stars do, but without enough mass to ignite the fusion of hydrogen into helium, the key thermonuclear reaction that keeps normal stars, such as our Sun, burning and giving off their own energy (Reid & Hawley 2005). [3] The cutoff is approximately 75-80 times the mass of Jupiter (MJ), where 1 Ms, or one solar mass, approximately 1048 MJ (Burrows et al. 2001). [4] As a result, these objects are technically not considered stars, but rather they straddle the border between stars and planets. [5] The tiny amount of light that they do give off is due primarily to a brief, youthful spurt of fusing deuterium (a heavier form of hydrogen) and lithium, and from the energy created by gravitational contraction (Reid & Hawley 2005).

The field ("stellar astronomy") is indicated in sentence 1 and the introduction of central terminology ("brown dwarfs") as early as sentence 2. Solomon introduces additional notation, as well as several recent sources on his research topic, in the remaining sentences.

Annotated Example of a Final Introductory Paragraph

from Paul M. Kominers's "Chip-Firing Analysis of Stabilization Behaviors, Hitting Times and Candy-Passing Games": *Semifinalist, Siemens Competition; Semifinalist, Intel Science Talent Search; Finalist, Intel International Science and Engineering Fair; Third Place, Karl Menger Prize; published in part in Pi Mu Epsilon Journal 12(8), 2008, pg. 459-460; MIT Class of 2012*

> [1] Past research has focused on properties of chip-firing, as well as the ending configurations produced by certain starting configurations (see [4, 5, 7, 8, 9]). [2] In this paper we develop formulae to count the number of firings required to stabilize maximized cycles and trees with one additional chip. [3] We present applications of these ideas to hitting time analysis. [4] We also examine a special chip-firing game called the "candy-passing game," and show that when the number of chips is at least 3n-2, where n is the number of vertices, the configuration will eventually become fixed. [5] We also give a conjecture extending this result and discuss this result's application to the PageRank algorithm.

This introduction both summarizes the results of the paper and distinguishes these results from the prior work on the topic. Although the specifics of the "candy-passing game" are deferred until later exposition (sentence 4), the statement of the result for this game is still placed in context.

Guts

Although the abstract and introduction will usually be the most widely read sections of the paper, the "guts" of the paper—the sections between the introduction and references—are the most important, from a technical standpoint. In these "guts" the author must report the entire content of the research.

The format of the "guts" often follows the order of the scientific method (see Chapter 11). Indeed, research papers should touch upon the hypotheses or questions investigated, methods of investigation, observations and results. A typical scientific paper will allocate a section or more to each of these categories and it is often prudent to present the material in the order of investigation.

However, fields often have their own standards of presentation. For example, theoretical fields often exclusively partition sections by topic, rather than by stages of investigation. Likewise, journals often have varying requirements for organization of content. Thus, it is essential that the author be familiar with the organizational standards of papers in his or her own field. Luckily, these standards can be observed while the author collects background materials for discussion in the introduction. This highlights an important, general lesson: *a student should read academic papers not only in order to learn their contents but also to become familiar with their style and organization.*

When writing the guts of the paper, the author should pay close attention to form and language. Scientific disciplines usually adopt a concise linguistic style. Additionally, some grammatical constructs usually discouraged in English writing are encouraged in scientific articles. For example, the passive voice is used regularly in experimental articles. As another example, we often see instances of the first person plural ("we") used in mathematics papers.

The author should again pay attention to ensure that all relevant terminology is defined, even if it is introduced in the later sections of the paper. He or she should also make sure to split block paragraphs, break textual monotony and to highlight the most important methods and results of the paper. Most importantly, he or she should remember to cite appropriately.

"I learned to write a scientific paper by reading previously published papers."
Lauren R. Lisann: *Finalist, Intel Science Talent Search; Semifinalist, Siemens Competition; Winner, American Academy of Neurology Neuroscience Research Prize; Yale Class of 2012*

"Nothing can beat the act of actually reading previously published papers and analyzing how the research is presented."
Dayan Li: *Intel Foundation Young Scientist, Intel International Science and Engineering Fair; Semifinalist, Intel Science Talent Search, Harvard Class of 2011*

"The materials and methods section for any field will differ, but generally this section should be a good description of the major procedures and tools that were used to complete the project. This section should be written in third person and should be very concise. Elaborate details are not necessary, but there should be enough information so that other scientists can repeat the procedure. The best thing to do is to look at the materials and methods section of a paper from your field."
Carol Y. Suh: *Finalist, Intel Science Talent Search; Third Place in Medicine and Health; Harvard Class of 2011*

Conclusion

While the conclusion of a professional research paper is often condensed into a single paragraph, that of a science fair paper may often be a full page or longer. Despite these differences it is essential that the research paper conclusion be as brief as possible.

The conclusion's main purpose is to underscore the importance of the results. It should contextualize the results of the project for the reader. It should be able to stand alone. Moreover, it should recall the last paragraph of the introduction and answer the reader's implicit question, "So what?"

The conclusion may also discuss open questions or directions for future research. While this is less common in academic papers, it is essential in science fair papers. (Many science fair judges perceive knowledge of open questions to be indicative of maturity within the field.)

References

At the end of the paper, the author should include a list of references. These should only include sources cited within the paper and should only include professional, academic sources. Sources such as Wikipedia are never acceptable as references in professional academic papers. (There is, of course, an exception to this rule: papers directly concerned with Wikipedia or its dynamics.)

It is also unacceptable for an author to cite a reference he or she has not seen, even if the reference is in another language. A citation is interpreted as a signature, indicating that the author has viewed the reference and verified that it contains the cited information. This is the presumption of both journal referees and judges, and it is academically dishonest to abuse this presumption. In some cases, science fair judges may actually ask students about specific references in order to test students' knowledge.

On a technical note, references should be formatted according to the preferred reference format of the intended venue. Most journals and conferences have their own unique formats for references and citations. Science fairs generally accept any reference format accepted within the research field, such as the MLA or APA formats.

MLA Format Example Journal Article Citation

> Smith, Gregor W. "Japan's Phillips Curve Looks Like Japan." Journal of Money, Credit and Banking 40.6 (2008): 1325-1326.

APA Format Example Journal Article Citation

> Renteln, P. and Dundes, A. (2005). Foolproof: A sampling of mathematical folk humor. Notices of the American Mathematical Society, 52(1), 24-34.

Attribution

Not as much of a section as a process, "attribution" differs from the "references" discussed above. Just as it is necessary to cite any relevant external sources, it is necessary for the author to acknowledge the contributions of others to the research.

In many fields, this attribution takes the form of co-authorship. Labs, for example, often list all the contributors to the work as authors and in some cases specify their respective contributions. In other fields, it may be more appropriate to attribute these contributions in an acknowledgments section at the end of the paper. It is also essential to acknowledge financial support from research grants or summer programs; these are often acknowledged in special footnotes on the title page.

Students should seek guidance from their research mentors regarding attribution. The mentor will assuredly know the etiquette of the field. Also, as the mentor may indicate, the proper forms of attribution typically differ between the publication and science fair drafts of the research paper.

Abstract

Although it is the first component of the paper, the abstract should be written last. The abstract of a research paper should be short (at most 250 words), clear and technical. It should emphasize the results of the project and underscore their importance.

Science fair abstracts are often quite different from publication-form abstracts. In particular, science fair abstracts often require background and contextual material that is often omitted in professional abstracts.

There is an art to writing abstracts, which may be gleaned from reading through examples. Thus, a few examples will help to illustrate:

Abstract

from Jacob Sanders's "Glucocorticoid regulation of cell survival in normal and cytokine-treated gastric chief cells": *Semifinalist, Intel Science Talent Search; Research Science Institute Top Paper Award; Harvard Class of 2009*

> Gastric chief cells secrete pepsinogen and are found at the base of gastric glands. Chief cells constitutively express the anti-apoptotic protein Bcl-xL, which may enable them to live longer than other gastric cells. We reveal that the cytokines

released as part of the inflammatory response during Helicobacter pylori infection dose-dependently disrupt chief cell monolayer integrity and viability. We also show that glucocorticoids dose-dependently increase expression of Bcl-xL, and hypothesize that this accounts for the ability of glucocorticoids to protect chief cells from cytokine-induced cell death. In addition, we show that glucocorticoids restrict the ability of cytokines to damage chief cell monolayer integrity. Finally, we propose two mechanisms by which cytokines overwhelm the protective ability of glucocorticoids, resulting in chief cell deletion and gastric atrophy during Helicobacter pylori infection.

Abstract

from Megan M. Blewett's "A Geostatistical Analysis of Possible Spirochetal Involvement in Multiple Sclerosis and Other Related Diseases": *Seventh Place, Intel Science Talent Search; First Place, Young Epidemiology Scholars Competition; Harvard Class of 2011*

Zoonotic diseases, especially those with insect or arthropod vectors, are recognized public health problems. This class of diseases includes West Nile Virus, Human Granulocytic Ehrlichiosis (HGE), Babesiosis, Rocky Mountain Spotted Fever and Lyme Disease. This study examines whether Multiple Sclerosis (MS), which is the most common primary neurological disorder of young adults, also belongs in this category. Visual and geostatistical analyses of MS and Lyme reveal striking similarities between the two diseases. Maps displaying each disorder's geographic distribution by county reveal this overlap visually. In addition, the statistical correlation between MS and Lyme deaths (specifically all arthropod-borne disease deaths) is significant at the state-level and highly significant at the county-level. MS incidence is known to vary with latitude; the study's statistical analysis reveals that Lyme Disease follows the same trend. Discussion of possible biological explanations of these geographical and statistical trends is included in this article. Significant correlations also exist with other diseases: on the state level, the correlation between MS and breast cancer is 0.330, and between MS and ALS (Motor Neuron Disease used in this study), the value is 0.618. The control, external accident/injury, did not yield significant correlations. Producing the maps and data required contacting all of the state epidemiologists in the nation for Lyme incidence data. Compiling the data has resulted in one of the most comprehensive Lyme databases available to researchers. The results of the visual, geostatistical and biochemical analyses suggest common spirochetal involvement in MS and related diseases.

Abstract

from Brett A. Harrison's "On the Reducibility of Cyclotomic Polynomials over Finite Fields": *Davidson Fellow; Research published in The American Mathematical Monthly 114(9), 2007, pg. 813-818; Harvard Class of 2010*

The irreducibility of a polynomial in a prime modulus implies irreducibility over the rationals. However, the converse is certainly not true. In fact, there are some polynomials that are irreducible over the rationals yet reducible in every prime modulus. We show that the nth cyclotomic polynomial reduces modulo all primes if and only if the discriminant of the nth cyclotomic polynomial is a square. We pose further questions about the specific factorization of cyclotomic polynomials over finite fields in relation to the discriminant.

Typesetting

The research paper should be carefully and clearly typeset. Although traditional word processing programs are acceptable for this purpose, the use of typesetting software is strongly recommended. Mathematics papers should always be typeset with LaTeX. Most other fields' papers can also benefit greatly from the slick appearance, formatting flexibility and high production quality of such typesetting software.

The paper venue (e.g., journals or science competitions) will provide exact typesetting or formatting instructions. Many venues require double-spaced, 12-point Times New Roman font on pages with one-inch margins, but the specific guidelines should be checked before submitting.

After initial typesetting, all authors and the research mentor should examine the paper for textual errors (and, of course, for errors in content). For each stage of revisions, an additional file should be kept for version control.

Publishing the Paper

Selecting the Venue

Once the paper is written, revised and thoroughly proofread, it is nearly ready for submission. The final step, choosing the venue, is essential and cannot be made in haste.

Papers are not only published in journals. They also appear in conference proceedings, books and lists of extended abstracts. Just as each field has its own preferred formats and guidelines, each field has its own publication process. In some fields, articles are sent to journals directly. In others they are first submitted to and presented at conferences, then aggregated into proceedings and then published in journals. As in many situations, then, the mentor is the best adviser when it comes to selecting the venue

An aside: Neither colleges nor science fairs distinguish substantially between these varied forms of publication. Any and all forms of peer-reviewed publication are impressive additions to a student's credentials.

Formatting

As has been mentioned, many journals have their own specialized formats. Before submission, the article should be entirely reformatted to match the journal's style guidelines. After this reformatting, the article should once again be proofread and reviewed by all authors.

Submission

Once the paper has been composed, formatted, checked and re-checked, it is ready for submission. The paper should be submitted by a "corresponding author," who will handle communications with the publisher. Oftentimes, this author is the research mentor or lab director, rather than the student.

Nonetheless, it often falls to the student to ensure that the paper is completely submitted.

Academic peer-review typically requires months, if not years. Still, the submission of the research work serves as a useful signal of quality. Indeed, some science fairs (such as the Siemens competition) ask whether the research has been submitted for publication.

If the paper is accepted, then the process will take over itself—the authors will usually make small textual revisions and then the article will be published. Although in some fields paper publication of an article may occur years after the article's acceptance, most journals publish advance-access copies online.

If the paper is rejected, then the authors should not lose heart! Rejection of papers is not uncommon, even for experienced professionals. Furthermore, rejection is often the fault of the refereeing process, rather than of the authors. In this case, the mentor should be contacted immediately; he or she can often evaluate the referee's comments and suggest a second choice of venue.

Take-Home Points

• Publication of research is critical!
• The instructions of this chapter are guidelines, not rules.
• The abstract should emphasize the results of the project and underscore their importance and should be the last section the author writes.
• The introduction should define relevant technical terminology, place the research work in context, indicate the work's importance and lay out the structure of the paper.
• References should only include sources cited within the paper and moreover the author of the paper should have read all the references cited.
• Acknowledgement of collaborators and funding sources is essential. The student should seek the mentor's advice regarding the relevant standards of attribution.
• A student should read academic papers not only in order to learn their contents but also to become familiar with their style and organization.
• A paper's conclusion should be able to stand alone.

13

General Presentation Techniques

Most rules of good writing apply to oral presentations as well. Whether sitting at your desk or standing in front of a blackboard, clarity should be your objective. And simplicity is always the best means of achieving it.
William Thomson, *Professor of Economics at the University of Rochester, in his A Guide for the Young Economist (p. 71)*

Communication is essential for scientific progress, hence researchers at all levels are called upon to present their work. It is therefore essential that scientific researchers develop effective presentation styles early in their careers. Indeed, student researchers should hone their presentation skills at least as much as they practice their lab techniques.

This chapter presents recommendations for the design and planning of presentations. The discussion explains how to plan for several important aspects of the presentation: the *audience* and *time limits*. Next, the selection and organization of presentation materials are discussed.

Neither *show boards* nor *slides* are discussed in this chapter, as the discussion here does not cover specific presentation formats. These two types of visual aid are discussed in Chapters 13 and 14, respectively.

Audience

Above all else, the presenter must know his or her audience. A technical presentation given before an audience of non-specialists will appear unclear and confusing, irrespective of the quality of the presentation or its content. Conversely, a presentation prepared for a general audience may appear immature to an audience of specialists.

"Knowing the audience" requires not only knowing the expected backgrounds of the audience members, but also understanding the physical constraints of the venue. For example, the presenter must prepare his or her posture, voice modulation and organization to match the physical area in which he or she will present.

Furthermore, the presenter must be appropriately dressed. This does not mean that he or she should match the attire of the audience members—he or she should exceed it! Professional scientists often attend talks in lab wear or in other casual attire. Nonetheless, the student presenter's clothing must set the presenter apart from the audience, conveying dignity and command. Typically, a male student should wear a suit, and a female student should wear either a suit or a business-casual dress skirt. Under no circumstances is it acceptable to present in jeans.

If in doubt about the dress requirements of the presentation venue, the presenter should aim for the upper limit. As a rule of thumb: *it is easier to remove a tie than to put one on.*

In general, the audience of a science research presentation will fall into one of three categories: *specialists in the presenter's field, general audiences,* or *scientists in other fields.*

Presentations for specialists in the presenter's field are the easiest to prepare. Before these audiences, the presenter must briefly summarize background material but should quickly move into an explanation of the presenter's actual work. The majority of the presentation should discuss the actual research and its contribution to the field. Most importantly, the presentation must distinguish the work from prior research. It is still necessary that the presenter explain technical definitions, but most basic definitions can be omitted.

In contrast, presentations before general audiences should almost never include technical details. The goal of such talks is to give an idea of the purpose, method and scope of the research work. This does not mean, *a priori,* that the entire project should be presented. It is often appropriate for a general-audience presentation to introduce the field, explain the purpose of the work and then detail a particularly interesting result. Most presentations of this type should include pictures or diagrams; they may also explain concepts through metaphor or analogy.

Scientists in other fields—professionals without background in the presenter's research area—are difficult to gauge in advance. (Unfortunately, a non-specialist scientist audience is expected at almost every science fair presentation.) A presentation before non-specialist scientists should provide a large amount of background material. However, the presenter should prepare to cover this background material quickly if it appears that the audience is more advanced than expected.

When presenting before a mixed audience, the presenter should plan to aim the majority of his or her presentation at the audience members with the least preparation. The specialists in the audience will understand and appreciate this choice.

Rules of Thumb

Evgenia Sendova, Coordinator of the Research Science Institute and Associate Professor at the Institute of Mathematics and Informatics of the Bulgarian Academy of Sciences, has an excellent, if humorous, rule of thumb for preparing an audience-appropriate presentation:

1. Everyone in the audience should understand the beginning of the presentation;
2. Most audience members should understand the middle of the presentation;
3. Nobody (not even the presenter) should understand the very end of the presentation.

Professor Sendova's advice succinctly sums up the outline of a quality research presentation. The presentation should begin with the work's background and broad impacts, introductory material which is clear and exciting to the entire audience. Then, the presentation should illustrate the research results at a level appropriate for the majority of the audience. Finally, the presentation should close with the "future" of the research problem, a discussion of open questions to which even the presenter does not know the answer.

Another rule of thumb is even simpler: The presenter should watch the audience and be dynamic. The presenter should speed up if the audience looks bored and slow down if the audience looks confused.

> "I have never completely memorized a presentation word for word, and always tailor it depending on a particular audience. For instance, I may decide to talk about different background research or go more in depth about particular methods or results."
> **Lauren R. Lisann:** *Finalist, Intel Science Talent Search; Semifinalist, Siemens Competition; Winner, American Academy of Neurology Neuroscience Research Prize; Yale Class of 2012*

Time Limits

Presenters should never exceed the time limit set for the presentation. To that end, it is essential that the presentation be planned and practiced in advance to ensure timely completion during the actual talk. Presenters should also know their speech habits in advance: Will they speed up or slow down when giving the actual presentation "under pressure?"

It is always better to run under the time limit than to run overtime. Extra time at the end of the presentation may be used for questions. In fact, the extra time may be the only time allotted for questions; the presenter should ascertain in advance whether this is the case.

> "Take your time. Find an optimal information/time ratio. Too slow is infinitely better than too fast."
> **Greg Brockman:** *Sixth Place, Intel Science Talent Search; Semifinalist, Siemens Competition; Finalist, Junior Science and Humanities Symposium; MIT Class of 2012*

Material

The presenter should always know his or her material. While it is appropriate to have detailed technical notes nearby during the talk, it is never appropriate to present from notes or from a script. Similarly, the presenter should have memorized the structure and organization of all his/her visual aids—no presentation aid should distract or detract from the fluidity of the presentation.

Furthermore, "knowing material" not only requires understanding the material covered in the talk, but also requires having working knowledge of back ground and supporting material. The presenter should be fluent in the language of his or her own work and should be able to field questions on any part of the project.

> "This is your research project. You should know more about it than anyone else in the world, so it should be easy to talk about."
> **Jacob Steinhardt:** *Third Place, Siemens Competition; Semifinalist, Intel Science Talent Search; MIT Class of 2012*

The Unbreakable Rule

As important as it is for the presenter to know what he or she "did" in the research work, it is even more important that the presenter know what he or she did not do. When fielding a question to which he or she does not know the answer, the presenter should never report a definitive response. In response to questions of theory or extension of the work, the presenter may postulate an idea. However, when unsure of the answer to a question of background, the presenter should never make up an answer—even if the questioner does not know the answer, some other member of the audience might.

> "Speak clearly and articulately, be concise and don't try to go beyond your capabilities."
> **Shravani Mikkilineni:** *Finalist, Intel Science Talent Search; Regional Finalist, Siemens Competition; Second Place in Medicine and Health/Mathematics, Intel International Science and Engineering Fair; Harvard Class of 2012*

> "If a judge asks you a question and you don't know the answer, just say 'I don't know,' and then, if you feel comfortable (and if possible), offer a possible explanation to their question."
> **Amber Hess:** *First Place in Chemistry, Intel International Science and Engineering Fair; Finalist, Intel Science Talent Search; Semifinalist, Siemens Competition; MIT Class of 2009*

Relationship Between the Presentation and the Research Paper

The "content" of a science research presentation is partially determined by the field's conventions and the difficulty of the material. However, as we have discussed, the venue and presentation format substantially impact the information to be included.

The presentation's organization should loosely follow the structure of the research paper (see Chapter 12, especially the section on "Content"). Nonetheless, good presentations eschew technical terminology whenever possible–this is in stark contrast to the research paper, which uses technical language as necessary.

Additionally, presentations typically include generous acknowledgments. Labs, coworkers and sponsors must be mentioned; audiences are sometimes thanked as well. Formal citations are usually unnecessary in presentations, as the audience will not have time to read a "references" section. However, informal citations (such as attribution) of prior work are essential.

Finally, the presenter must remember that even a good presentation can only skim the surface of the material. A reader may read the research paper indefinitely; a presentation may not exceed a fixed time limit. Some details will therefore have to be omitted from the presentation in favor of sketches or simplified explanations. To this end, figures and charts provide excellent presentation aids as they summarize information.

Take-Home Points

- The presenter must know his or her audience.
- When presenting before a mixed audience, the presenter should plan to aim the majority of his or her presentation at the audience members with the least preparation.
- The presenter should watch the audience and be dynamic.
- The presenter should never exceed the time limit. It is always better to run under the time limit than to run overtime.
- When unsure of the answer to a question of background, the presenter should never make up an answer!
- Even a good presentation can only skim the surface of the material.

14

Making a Professional Show Board or Poster

The visual aid is not the main event—the role of the visual aid is to illustrate or emphasize what you say.
D. Eric Walters, *Professor of Biochemistry & Molecular Biology, Rosalind Franklin University, and* Gale Climenson Walters, *in their Scientists Must Speak: Bringing Presentations to Life (p. 38)*

A *show board* is a freestanding, visual presentation aid, often consisting of several panels of information. While similar in content to a show board, a *poster* is usually a single panel which must be mounted for display. Show boards are required in the later stages of most science fairs (e.g., The Siemens Competition, the Intel Science Talent Search and the Intel International Science and Engineering Fair), while posters are regularly required for local presentations and academic conferences.

This chapter discusses how to construct both of these visual aids, following the presentation model of Chapter 13, "General Presentation Techniques." The visual aid design process occurs in three steps: *content selection, layout* and *construction.* To ensure a quality product, these procedures must be conducted sequentially; the following sections address each step in turn. These steps will also form the core of the discussion of *slides* in the next chapter.

Content Selection

The content of a show board or poster should loosely follow the guidelines for presentation content outlined in Chapter 13, "General Presentation Techniques." It is essential that the visual aid's content supplement a carefully organized presentation. Therefore, the presentation should be planned before the board design process begins. While judges will look at the visual aid, they will focus on the presenter.

The visual aid should directly address the primary audience of the presentation. However, unlike some presentation aids, show boards and posters offer an opportunity to present flexible content in presentation settings where the audience members are of varying scientific backgrounds. A presentation need not refer to every inch of the show board or poster, hence the content may comprehensively address background, methods, results, conclusions and references. The content may even include some technical information which will be inaccessible to some audience members.

A good, simple guideline for content selection is to imagine that the show board or poster is a research paper converted into a presentation aid. Unlike the paper, however, the display is only an aid. The structure should usually be skeletal—bullets may replace paragraphs and dense technical material should be elided. However, this is not a rigid rule. Indeed, dense block paragraphs are sometimes standard fare. (This is especially true for professional conference posters.) To ensure that the content density level is appropriate, the presenter should study examples from the intended presentation venue. Additionally, the research mentor may be able to provide advice in this regard.

A presenter should expect to gesture to his or her show board or poster during the talk, but should not expect the judges to read block text during the presentation. (Additionally, he or she should certainly not need to read the visual aid's text while presenting!) However, judges at most science fairs will read the show boards in advance of the presentation session, instead of reading the presenters' papers. Likewise, poster presentations often have a session in which the posters are displayed without presenters. Thus, although it serves a secondary role during the actual presentation, the visual aid must be able to stand alone, including important material such as definitions, motivation, key equations and results. Additionally, the visual aid should include labeled figures and tables whenever possible. These intrinsically visual elements enliven the aid and are easy to refer to during presentation.

> "It's important to realize that the poster board is not an enlarged research paper—there's no need to include and explain everything."
> **Dayan Li:** *Intel Foundation Young Scientist, Intel International Science and Engineering Fair; Semifinalist, Intel Science Talent Search; Harvard Class of 2011*

Layout

The visual aid should be aesthetically pleasing and conceptually clear. It should stand out and add excitement and energy to the presentation. Nonetheless, show boards and posters should be minimalist—if the intended design cannot be sketched, then it is probably too complicated.

Thus, the most important suggestion for visual aid layout is that the aid should be designed on paper before construction. This will enforce careful planning and will also help to ensure that layout decisions are attentive to the intended dimensions of the final product.

Dimensions

Since layout relies on the visual aid's dimensions, it is important to decide on these dimensions early. Sometimes, visual aid dimensions will be specified by the presentation venue. (This is especially common for academic conference poster presentations, which usually require specific poster dimensions.)

However, some science fairs give no guidance regarding dimensions. Consequently, science fair show boards seem to grow taller every year. Nonetheless, a show board with text reaching substantially higher than the presenter's eye-level is ineffective. During the presentation, focus should be directed towards the presenter's face. Excessively tall show boards may therefore be distracting or—worse—disorienting.

One safe way to add height and visual appeal to a show board is to add a title bar above the show board proper. Many show board manufacturers sell panels which may be used for this purpose. Placing the title above the rest of the show board actually improves the presentation environment, getting the title out of the way of the presentation content.

Organization

Like papers, most show board and poster displays are organized in modules which separate the key elements of the presentation. For example, visual content might be organized into *background, hypotheses, methods, data, results, conclusions* and *future research* modules. Presentation modules should be separated visually, either by matting or by headers. The layout should be consistent across modules, so that the visual aid coheres aesthetically. (For example, presenting modules in distinct fonts is discouraged.) These divisions are functional as well as practical: When presenting before an expert, the presenter might choose to omit the "background" section from his or her discussion. Modular organization makes it easy to recover the presentation organization after such a decision.

> "The board should be professional looking, clean-cut and easy to read. There should be a logical path from your abstract to your conclusion."
> **Amber Hess:** *First Place in Chemistry, Intel International Science and Engineering Fair; Finalist, Intel Science Talent Search; Semifinalist, Siemens Competition; MIT Class of 2009*

> "Sometimes it is easy to get caught up in making a board that's fancy. In the end, what really matters is how well you display your research. Try to make your board simple and elegant; there should be a flow to the way your work is presented."
> **Meredith MacGregor:** *Intel Foundation Young Scientist, Intel International Science and Engineering Fair; Ninth Place, Intel Science Talent Search; Harvard Class of 2011*

Coloration

A show board's background color generally should be black or white. Both colors are available at most office supply stores and can also be ordered online.

Other show board colors are available, as well, but should almost never be used. Muted background colors may help the show board stand out, but bright background prints generally distract from the presentation content and may appear immature.

Color should be used sparingly within the board, to supplement the visual aid's content. Variations in color may highlight specific information. One excellent application of color is matting: different modules may be matted on single-color mattes and then mounted. However, the presenter must ensure that colored and color-matted text is legible at a small distance. Furthermore, matte colors should be muted and should not distract from the text.

Use of Figures

As mentioned earlier, figures are excellent additions to a visual aid. They should be placed near their associated modules and mounted in a fashion consistent with the rest of the layout. If matting is used, figures are often matted separately from text blocks.

The presenter should expect to gesture to figures during the presentation. Nonetheless, all figures on a show board or poster should be captioned for completeness. The figures should be sized according to importance and space availability. In general, figures should appear at least twice as large in the visual aid as in the paper—they will need to be viewed at a distance.

Finally, a caveat: while figures make a presentation exciting, they should be featured only if relevant. Clip art and humorous images should never appear in formal presentations. Even scientific images should not be featured if they will not be discussed in the presentation.

Use of Tables

Like figures, tables increase the visual excitement of a show board or poster. Additionally, tables often contain crucial data or results.

Tables are notoriously difficult to read—especially at presentation distance. A listener will be able to follow at most three or four rows of a table during the presentation. Thus, large tables are usually ineffective. If a large table must be included, its most relevant rows and columns should be clearly demarcated, either via bold text or color highlighting.

Additionally, table fonts must be large enough to be read at a distance. The text of the table should usually be as large as the visual aid's other text and may be larger.

Physical Aids

While the show board or poster serves as a visual aid, some science fairs allow *physical aids* which may be displayed in front of a show board. These should always include a copy of the formal research paper. Additionally, physical aids might include scale models, lab materials or other demonstrative items associated with the research project.

Other than the research paper, physical aids must be directly relevant to the presentation. Otherwise, they will simply distract from the presentation and show board.

Construction

While construction is more mechanical than the other two steps of visual aid design, it is essential and must be undertaken with precision. Slipshod construction can render a brilliantly planned visual aid unprofessional and ineffective. (By analogy, although experiments are often mechanical, imprecision in experimentation renders even brilliant experimental design useless.)

Typesetting

As with papers (see Chapter 12) and slides (see Chapter 15), visual aid content should be carefully and clearly typeset. Traditional word processing programs are acceptable for this purpose. However, proper use of typesetting or design software can drastically improve the quality of the visual aid.

Although many word processors include equation formatting modes, equations created with these programs rarely scale well. At poster size, they thin out and are difficult to read. By contrast, LaTeX formulae are scale-invariant and hold their figures even at poster size.

Show board panels and poster layouts may be formatted with professional design programs. While use of design programs requires practice, computerized layouts are easy to modify and reorganize—this is helpful during the construction process, since gauging space usage exactly is often difficult.

> "To make a professional board or poster, one ought to use a professional-quality software package."
> **Greg Brockman:** *Sixth Place, Intel Science Talent Search; Semifinalist, Siemens Competition; Finalist, Junior Science and Humanities Symposium; MIT Class of 2012*

Printing

When possible, the visual aid should be printed with non-smudging ink, on high-quality paper. A laser printer will suffice for this purpose. (Inkjet and dot-matrix printers should be avoided.) Either matte or gloss finishing may be appropriate; this decision usually is not specified by the presentation venue and is therefore an aesthetic choice. Above all, however, is the imperative that the visual aid's text be legible; this requisite should guide all finishing decisions.

Most copy or fax stores and some laboratories have poster printers. These should be used for conferences; the research mentor can advise if and when professional poster printing is appropriate. Poster printers may also be used for show board modules or panels, but this may be more complicated than a combination of laser printing and careful measurement.

Mounting

If visual components are printed separately, then there is a "mounting" stage of construction, in which these components are combined to form the show board or poster.

All visual and textual lines should be straight and parallel to the top of the display. Margins between modules should be equal and standardized across the board, as should margins between show board panels. Both a paper cutter and a T-square may be required to ensure precision in this process. These tools may be obtained at hardware stores and may also be available in laboratories.

Spray adhesive or some other full-coverage adhesive should be used to affix modules. This will help to prevent air bubbles from forming. However, these adhesives are often indelible, so they should not be applied before the visual aid content and layout is finalized.

Take-Home Points

- A show board or poster should directly address the primary audience of the presentation. However, flexible content should be included in presentation settings where the audience members are of varying scientific backgrounds.
- Relevant figures and tables often are excellent additions to a show board or poster.
- A show board or poster should be able to stand alone.
- Any visual aid should be designed on paper before construction.
- Color should be used sparingly within a visual aid and only to supplement the aid's content.
- While construction is more mechanical than the other steps of visual aid design, it is essential and must be undertaken with precision.

15

Giving a Winning Slide Presentation

In my mind's eye, I visualize how a particular . . . sight and feeling will appear on a print. If it excites me, there is a good chance it will make a good photograph.
Ansel Adams

Unlike show boards and posters, *slides* are sequentially displayed visual aids which appear only in connection with a presentation. The most significant difference between slides and most other visual aids is that slides are never read alone. Slides are required in the final stages of many science fairs (e.g., the Siemens Competition, the Intel Science Talent Search and the Junior Sciences and Humanities Symposium) and are also standard fare at academic conferences and symposia.

A chapter on visual aids benefits greatly from visual aids. To this end, the Guide website contains a repository of example slides. While many of these examples were constructed before the authorship of this *Guide*, they are all of exemplary quality and supplement the *Guide's* discussion.

> "Like a poster presentation, a PowerPoint presentation should be concise, colorful (but not gaudy or kaleidoscopic) and should serve only as a place to start off your presentation, a place to refer back to (i.e., graphs, tables, etc.) and a visual roadmap."
> **Dayan Li:** *Intel Foundation Young Scientist, Intel International Science and Engineering Fair; Semifinalist, Intel Science Talent Search; Harvard Class of 2011*

Content Selection

Slides are not freestanding visual aids. They are an arm of a presentation and must be crafted as such. Thus, while the presentation should be outlined in advance of the slide design process, the presentation's content should be fleshed out as the slide content is selected. The slides should directly address the primary audience of the presentation. They are inflexible presentation aids—every audience member will see every slide.

Slide content is always distracting, temporarily drawing focus away from the presenter. Consequently, full sentences should be included sparingly (if ever) and all citations should be abbreviated. Presentation slides should never include complicated or irrelevant information. In particular, slides should rarely include technical content, even if the audience is expected to have a technical background.

Slides should serve as an outline and figure repository. They should include key definitions, methods, figures and results. Unlike the research paper, the presentation slides need not address the full scope of the research; they might instead focus on especially pertinent examples or easily understood results.

A presenter should engage with his or her slides during the presentation, perhaps gesturing with a laser pointer. Although presenters are often tempted to use the outline format of the slides as a crutch, the presenter should have his/her presentation and slide order memorized, so that he or she need only glance at the slides during the presentation. Judges and audience members, by contrast, will read every word of the slides; each slide should therefore dynamically reinforce the content of the presentation.

> "Do not simply read text off of slides; as with free-standing boards, less text is generally better, as long as you have prepared your speech."
> **Lauren R. Lisann:** *Finalist, Intel Science Talent Search; Semifinalist, Siemens Competition; Winner, American Academy of Neurology Neuroscience Research Prize; Yale Class of 2012*

Layout

Slides will usually be displayed with a projector. Thus, they will appear several times larger than the presenter's height. Since the audience's focus should be drawn to the presenter as often as possible, slides must be minimalist.

Careful attention should be paid to presentation length. Most slides take at least a minute to display and discuss completely. The presentation slides should be "storyboarded" on paper in advance, to ensure that their progression flows reasonably and that their design is not inordinately complex. (As in Chapter 13: a visual aid design which cannot be reasonably sketched on paper is too complicated.)

Macro-Organization

Following the "outline" formula, most slides should contain bulleted lists of phrases which will be expanded upon in the presentation. Again consistent with this model, slides should be ordered in a progression which follows the flow of ideas in the presentation. In many presentations, a preliminary "road map" slide which describes the overall presentation structure should be included.

Each slide should have a header which indicates the slide's content area (e.g., "Definitions," "Hypotheses," "Methods," "Results"). It is generally good for this progression to develop ideas linearly, beginning with background ideas and proceeding through experimental design, procedures and results.

Unless a competition explicitly forbids acknowledgments, it is essential to include an "acknowledgments" slide at the end of the presentation, acknowledging mentors, laboratories, teachers and funding support. This slide usually does not count against the time allowance; it can be displayed after the presentation is completed. Also, since it is the last slide of the presentation, it may be omitted at the last minute if acknowledgments do not seem to be in vogue at the presentation venue.

Micro-Organization

The slides should demonstrate consistent organization. Their layouts should all be identical; header formats, text and caption sizes should be uniform.

Slide background colors should not be distracting. White is always a safe choice; blacks, tans and pale blues are often acceptable as well. Likewise, text colors should be chosen so that the slides are legible, even at a large distance. Excessive use of colors—especially bright colors—will distract from the actual content of the presentation and might appear immature.

> "[T]he font should be readable and the colors [...] should be eye-catching but not irritating."
> **Boris Nikolaev Kolev:** *Sofia High School of Mathematics*

It is extraordinarily important that slides not be cluttered. The rule of thumb for measuring this is unequivocal: if a slide looks like it might be cluttered, then it is. Such slides should be broken down into multiple slides, with the time limits kept in mind.

Use of Overlays

Animations and videos should be used in formal presentations only if they are directly relevant to the presentation content (e.g., an animation of a chemical reaction). By contrast, clever use of overlays (appearing or disappearing slide content) can greatly improve a presentation. Since slide text is a distractor, it behooves the presenter to hide text before and after its discussion. However, a balance must be struck: if long text blocks disappear before the audience has the time to read them, then the audience will become confused.

A good rule of thumb is that information should appear in sequence. Each bullet or image should be hidden until its phase of the presentation. While text need not disappear after it is discussed, it may be beneficial for it to grey out, so that audience attention is always focused on the most recent addition. (Alternatively, short text blocks may simply disappear after they are presented.)

Use of Figures

Figures are nearly essential for slides. Even detailed figures can be viewed and interpreted upon projection and pointers may be used to direct audience attention toward sections of figures.

Although the presenter will explain the significance of each figure, a very short caption should be included which simply states the significance of the image and attributes the source.

Generally, each figure should be allotted its own slide. There are exceptions to this rule, however. For example, several figures might be used in a flowchart, or figures may be successively overlaid on a single slide to demonstrate changes in a situation

While humorous figures are appropriate for some audiences (such as classroom plenary talks), such images should never appear in formal presentations. As slides and presentations are closely linked, even scientific images should not be included if they will not be discussed in the presentation.

Use of Tables

Although tables usually contain crucial data or results, they are often unnecessary in slide presentations. Tables are typically complicated and are notoriously difficult for audience members to read during a verbal presentation.

Nonetheless, tables may be included sparingly. Used properly, they will add to the variety of the slides and provide an opportunity for clever overlay usage.

A listener will be able to follow at most three or four rows of a table during the presentation. Even within these limits, dynamic highlighting should be used to draw attention to specific features of the table. In particular, overlays should be used so that the relevant sections of the table are highlighted in the sequence in which the presentation addresses them.

Physical Aids

While the slides are the primary visual aid of a presentation, in rare cases it may be appropriate to include a physical aid. Usually, however, a picture or video of such an aid can be included in the slides, instead.

If a physical aid must be used, it should be held in front of the audience during the presentation and should not be passed around, as a passing object will provide a continuous distraction. If the presentation is to be held in a large room, this strategy will not work—most audience members will not be able to see the physical aid clearly. In such cases, physical aids should be avoided.

Construction

In the case of slides, "construction" refers to the processes of inputting content into slides and formatting the final product. "Construction" may also include conversion of slides to transparencies, in the case of talks which will not be projected from computers.

Construction processes are mechanical, but they must be carried out with utmost care and attention. Indeed, poor construction can render a brilliantly planned visual aid unprofessional and ineffective. (By analogy: although experiments are often mechanical, imprecision in experimentation renders even brilliant experimental design useless.)

Typesetting

As with papers (see Chapter 12) and show boards (see Chapter 13), visual aid content should be carefully and clearly typeset. Traditional word processing-level programs (such as PowerPoint) are acceptable for slide design. Professional slide typesetting software may also be used. Typesetting slides is tedious, but will often dramatically improve the final product.

Word-processing programs usually provide a wealth of overlay and formatting tools, which simplify slide design. However, slide-projection size equations are usually ugly and illegible unless typeset with professional typesetting tools.

If plastic overhead projector slides are to be used, these slides should be professionally generated from a PDF-formatted file.

The Slide File

After initial formatting, the slide show should be previewed and examined for flow and overlay errors. The slides' accuracies should be checked, both on a computer screen and on a paper printout.

The presentation venue may have instructions regarding the acceptable slide file formats. It is imperative that the presenter be aware of these instructions in advance—especially if plastic overhead projector slides are required.

At least three copies of the computerized slide file should travel to the presentation: two distinct copies should be saved on two distinct travel drives and a paper printout should be included, as well. (If plastic overhead projector slides are to be used, then two copies of these slides should be accompanied by a paper copy and a travel drive containing the original file.) The travel drives should be carried separately, one on the presenter's person, the other in his or her backpack or briefcase. The printout should not be used during the presentation, but should be used for rehearsal prior to the presentation. An additional copy of the final slide file should be stored in the presenter's email account.

Take-Home Points

- Slides should directly address the primary audience of the presentation.
- In slides:
  - full sentences should appear sparingly, if ever;
  - all citations should be abbreviated;
  - complicated or irrelevant information should be avoided;
  - figures are nearly essential; and
  - overlays and tables should be used cleverly—and sparingly.
- Most slides take at least a minute to display and discuss completely.
- Slides should follow the flow of ideas in the presentation, demonstrating consistent and uncluttered organization.
- Prior to the presentation, the presenter should prepare multiple copies of the slide file in an acceptable file format.

Part IV:
Opportunities and Competitions

16

Intel International Science and Engineering Fair

The true delight is in the finding out rather than in the knowing.
Isaac Asimov

Introduction

More than any other international high school science competition, ISEF fosters a cross-cultural and interdisciplinary exchange of science among many of the world's top young researchers. The scale of the competition is itself astounding: Over 1,600 students from nearly 60 countries, regions, and territories showcase their research over the course of a week. In the process, participants learn about not only other cutting-edge projects but also different cultures and languages. ISEF epitomizes the global communication of science, as students compete to effectively and persuasively present their research projects to the scrutinizing judges, their peers and the public.

A Peek Into a Winner's Personal Journey

In the summer of 2006, rising senior Dayan 'Jack' Li started an internship in the Laboratory of Pathology at the National Cancer Institute in Bethesda, Maryland. Empowered by the desire to learn about tumor growth and metastasis, he studied gene regulation in cancer angiogenesis, which is the growth of blood capillaries that provide the nutrients and the means for tumors to grow and spread. Unbeknownst to him, a year later, his summer work would earn him grand prizes in school and regional science fairs and catapult him into international spotlight as he became one of the three top winners in the 2007 Intel International Science and Engineering fair held in Albuquerque, New Mexico.

Winning ISEF was certainly a shock to the young aspiring scientist. Never had he fathomed the possibility of succeeding at a competition of that caliber, especially during his first few weeks in the lab, when baffling and sometimes contradictory data threatened to keep his project at standstill. Unfazed, Jack diligently worked to improve his technique and optimize data collection while keeping an open mind about unexpected results. Though at first it seemed he accomplished little at the end of the summer, upon closer data analysis and intensive background reading, he generated fascinating insights, which he made sure to emphasize to the judges at the Intel ISEF.

To him, the most valuable preparation for ISEF was honing his presentation skills and knowing his project inside-out. Countless impressive and award-worthy projects line the aisles in the ISEF exhibit hall. One of the factors that distinguishes award winners is the quality of their presentations. Jack used the various presentation techniques he learned over the course of his high school career to design an appealing poster board and deliver a compelling exposition about his work and its significance.

Arriving in Albuquerque, Jack did not set his mind on winning ISEF, but on doing his personal best to effectively communicate science and interact with all the other bright students. Though winning ISEF was definitely rewarding, the most lasting reward was his interaction with the scientific community and his exposure to the cutting-edge, multidisciplinary science. ISEF drastically broadened his perspective on biomedical research, as it showed him the endless possibilities of other fields besides cancer. As a result of ISEF, Jack, now a student at Harvard College, has decided to explore a research field completely foreign to him—developmental biology. Jack owes a considerable part of his scientific maturation to his eye-opening experience at ISEF.

ISEF—A Brief History

The International Science and Engineering Fair was founded in 1950 by the nonprofit organization Society for Science & the Public (SSP) (www. societyforscience.org). Based in Washington, D.C., SSP (previously known as Science Service) inaugurated the international science fair and has been its prime organizer ever since. As the only global event of its kind that aims to promote and showcase high school research, the ISEF has attracted the endorsement of the world's leading science corporations. In 1997, the Intel Foundation, acting through its Innovation for Education program, became the main sponsor of the event, which was subsequently renamed as the Intel International Science and Engineering Fair in honor of Intel's significant financial and promotional contributions to the science fair. Since then, multiple other science companies such as Agilent Technologies, Alcatel-Lucent and the Ricoh Corporation have joined as sponsors. These major corporations, along with over 70 other organizations, have provided generous scholarships, monetary grants, scientific trips and countless other opportunities for ISEF's staggering award repository, which totals more than $4 million dollars.

Every year, ISEF is held at a pre-selected host city in the United States. Over the past years, cities as diverse as Cleveland, Portland, Albuquerque and Atlanta have displayed their unique cultures and atmospheres to students across the United States and from all over the world. Roughly 1,600 students from approximately 50 countries compete in the week-long event, sharing both fascinating science and vibrant cultures. By recruiting leading scientists as its judges and attracting enormous media coverage, Intel ISEF is a singularly powerful convergence at the apex of young scientific research. Year after year, Intel ISEF recognizes and inspires new waves of aspiring scientific pioneers and inventors.

The road to ISEF

Eligibility

Intel ISEF is open exclusively to high school students. ISEF gathers students who have received top honors at one of the 550 affiliated regional science fairs across the world. Students often find themselves rising through the ranks in multiple smaller-scale science fairs (school, county, state and regional) before they are granted a spot at ISEF (i.e., before they become finalists). Due to this screening process, all those who partake in ISEF have exceptional projects and well practiced presentation skills. To search for an affiliated science fair, go to http://www.societyforscience.org/isef/students/aff_fairsearch.asp.

Paperwork and Documentation

Registering a project for ISEF and its affiliated fairs is not a trivial task. To be accepted, projects must obey stringent rules for research safety and procedures, especially when the research deals with hazardous materials, human subjects and other vertebrate animals. Multiple forms have to be completed and approved by a review committee before the project becomes eligible for the fair. The process can take weeks and, in rare cases, months. The ISEF Rules Wizard (http://societyforscience.org/isef/ students/wizard/index.asp) provides step-by-step instructions that guide you to the appropriate forms. Official ISEF abstracts also have to be submitted as part of the paperwork package. These abstracts will serve as official, ISEF-stamped summaries of your projects and will be made available to the public and the media. Hopefully, most of these logistical tasks will have been completed as part of the preparation for the affiliated regional science fairs, which should adhere to the ISEF guidelines.

Pre-fair Logistical Preparation

Though affiliated science fairs should all enforce ISEF regulations about safe and rigorous research practices, rules regarding backboards, displays, judging and other on-site rules may differ. Usually, students have more freedom to choose the form of project display at ISEF. In addition to being bigger than those at regional fairs, displays adopt a more creative variety. Although the majority still uses tall, enlarged backboards, a few students bring custom-made wooden boards with hinged extensions (to increase display area) and even lighting. Others have posters elegantly mounted on large stands. There is certainly no need for fancy presentations. Whichever way you opt to display your project, you should focus on portability and presentation.

Since the displays must be shipped to the science fair venue ahead of time, shipping only the unwieldy empty backboards first can be helpful. The actual poster and contents can be carried with the students in their travel so that they can assemble the display on-site (Velcro strips are an efficient and convenient way to attach the content to the display boards). Be sure to ship your boards early, as complications in shipping can occur. There is a designated period for project assembly at the beginning of ISEF. Even though there will be a supplies area at the fair, it is wise to bring the necessary assembly materials (scissors, tape, rulers, etc), as the materials quickly run out. To review the display guidelines and safety regulations, go to *http://societyforscience.org/isef/rules/safdisp.pdf*.

How to Succeed at ISEF

Although you have been progressively polishing your project throughout the previous science fairs, now is the time to make your display as appealing and your arguments as watertight as possible. You should have an idea of what needs improvement based upon the comments of local science fair judges and your peers. It may help to ask a research teacher, science fair coordinator or your mentor for suggestions on how to make the project more thorough, more communicable, more interesting and more appealing to both other scientists and the general public.

You will most likely not have sufficient time to gather and include additional data between your last science fair and ISEF, but the weeks preceding the event can be used to perform more background research about your project. At ISEF, knowing your project is not enough; you need to have a firm grasp of the most important research that led to your project and further understand both the scientific and social implications of your research. In order to test scientific aptitude, judges often ask questions that require participants to apply the information presented in the project to other experimental situations. By becoming even more familiar with the network of knowledge that connects your own work to other projects in related fields, you will be able to intelligently answer such questions.

It cannot be stressed enough: know your project inside out. This means being able to articulate the project's strengths and to recognize your project's weaknesses. While emphasizing the project's significance and innovation impresses the judges with the impact of your work, addressing the shortcomings of your research in a genuine and constructive manner shows your evaluators your scientific maturity. This is not to say that you should mention all the weaknesses of your project during your presentation, but be prepared to talk about such weaknesses and suggest solutions when judges point them out.

Finally, rehearse your oral presentation until you can deliver it naturally. Make a conscious effort to speak slowly, articulate each syllable of every word and clearly project your voice. The point of repetitive presentation practice is not to memorize a script word by word—this will ultimately hurt you more than benefit you—but to familiarize yourself with the train of thought involved in presenting your project in the most understandable and memorable way. Since student presenters have only ten minutes to make a good impression, painstakingly decide what to say and how to say it. Since your assigned judges will have previewed your posters and research papers the night before, they will be more interested in having a conversation with you rather than stand and listen to the story of your project from beginning to end—so be ready for interruptions. It is still essential to rehearse your presentation so that you can best emphasize important points and provide insights that the judges missed in their cursory previews of your project.

On the day of judging, the best way to do well is to stay relaxed. A lucid and calm mind is paramount to tackling the critical thinking questions judges can ask you. Therefore, quench the building anxiety by running through your mind the course of your oral presentation, the important points, the shortcomings and possible questions that judges might ask. When answering questions, it is perfectly acceptable to pause and think them through before formulating a thoughtful answer. If, after pondering for a while, you absolutely do not know the answer, it is also fine to tell them so. However, do not reply with just, "I don't know." Voice your thoughts, questions and guesses as you ponder about the question to demonstrate your problem-solving efforts. If the question concerns a fact or piece of information that you are not aware of, then tell the judges that you would like to do more research into that topic.

Ultimately, the key to success at Intel ISEF is not to focus on modifying the content of your presentation, but using every means to improve the communication of your work. Consider what aspect in your presentation will distinguish your project from all the other projects in the fair and what will make the judges remember your project and come back to scrutinize it further.

In the end, with all your prior preparation, there is no need to be nervous. Seize this opportunity to inspire others with your contribution to science and your passion for the project. The desire to win should not dominate your thoughts during ISEF. Shake off the tension and enjoy. The week is yours; the world is watching and regardless of the end results, you will enjoy lasting benefits.

"Be prepared for intense rounds of judging. Speak with clarity and confidence—judges always seem to like someone who is confident with what they are presenting. You will be given a limited amount of time to present months of research. So, be sure to give a concise presentation by introducing only important data and information."

Natalie Saranga Omattage: *Intel Foundation Young Scientist, Intel International Science and Engineering Fair; Semifinalist, Siemens Competition; University of Richmond Class of 2012*

"To do well, you need solid research that's creative, original, significant and that you did yourself. So my first advice concerns conducting the research. To start, I recommend thinking big and choosing an interesting and important problem that might make a real difference. Don't assume that just because you're in high school you can't do imaginative and significant research that might even alter the paradigms of your field. Then work as hard as you can planning and accurately doing the experiments, thinking broadly about your research and learning everything you can about it, through textbooks, journal articles and asking people and yourself questions.

To win at ISEF, you also need to be able to communicate to the judges, clearly and concisely, with enthusiasm and confidence, the essence of your research and how what you did yourself is creative and significant. I recommend to focus on the two or three most important aspects of your research and practice (a lot!) presenting it in 5-7 minutes, being careful to leave out extraneous details. Also, practice answering as many questions as you can think of (e.g., how did you get the idea for your research, what did you do, what are the error limitations, what problems did you have, etc.). You should also make sure you understand and can explain the scientific concepts underlying your research. In my experience, the judges keep questioning you with more and more challenging questions, trying to stump you."

Philip V. Streich: *Intel Foundation Young Scientist, Intel International Science and Engineering Fair; Third Place, Intel Science Talent Search; Regional Finalist, Siemens Competition; Davidson Fellow Laureate; United States Physics Olympiad Team; Harvard Class of 2013*

"Intel ISEF is an amazing experience. The first time I went, I was a little intimidated by how many people were there and how sophisticated all of the research was. I think that it's best to be confident in yourself and take pride in presenting your work. Be excited that you get to talk about your project with experts in the field. ISEF is a great way to get experience giving a scientific presentation, so enjoy the experience!"

Meredith MacGregor: *Intel Foundation Young Scientist, Intel International Science and Engineering Fair; Ninth Place, Intel Science Talent Search; Harvard Class of 2011*

Take-Home Points

• Intel ISEF is a unique opportunity for you to present your work internationally and interact with accomplished young scientists from all over the globe.
• Once eligible for ISEF, registering for the fair requires a considerable amount of paperwork, so complete the paperwork in advance to prevent unforeseen logistical problems.
• The most valuable preparation for ISEF is polishing both the visual and oral presentation.
• ISEF is more than just a competition; it is an international effort to inspire and share science by promising high school scientists.

17

Siemens Competition in Math, Science and Technology

It is not knowledge, but the act of learning, not possession but the act of getting there, which grants the greatest enjoyment.
Carl Friedrich Gauss

When you see a piece of metal being heated, let's say a cooking pot, do you ever wonder how the heat travels across the metal surface? And how that temperature can affect the surface of the metal? Well Michael Viscardi, an undergraduate at Harvard from San Diego, CA developed a project which could explain these questions when he was 16. He won the 2005 Siemens Competition in Math, Science and Technology and in the process received a $100,000 college scholarship. "I formed a theorem which characterizes all such domains for which the resulting solution is rational—namely in terms of their Riemann maps and their Bergman kernels," Viscardi said. Essentially, Viscardi improved a 19th century law by mathematician Lejeune Dirichlet. According to the Siemens Foundation, "Viscardi's research can lead to a better airplane wing design, better stabilization of the NASA space shuttle and high-speed rail transportation."

What is the Siemens Competition?

The Siemens Competition, formerly known as the Siemens Westinghouse Science Competition, is a prestigious research competition for high school seniors. Funded by the Siemens Foundation, this competition is also affiliated with the College Board. Unlike other science competitions, it is divided into two major categories: individual and team projects. The Siemens Competition focuses almost entirely on the research paper in contrast to ISEF and STS.

Competition Overview

First Phase: Application and Semi-Finals

There are three phases to the Siemens Competition. In order to be eligible for the individual project division, you must be a high school senior. If you are not a senior, you can still enter the team project division as part of a group of two or three fellow students which does not need to include a senior. You must submit your research report by the deadline, which is usually in early October. The entries are "blind read" by a panel of judges assembled by the College Board. Papers are judged solely by the quality of the research. It is important to note that the Siemens Competition application also asks if your paper has been submitted for publication. Therefore, if possible and appropriate, it may be helpful to submit your paper to a journal or conference by the time you enter the competition.

> "I would recommend writing a very thorough research paper. The judges score this competition solely on the information given to them in the paper. Be sure to include everything; assume that the judges have no prior knowledge on your research's subject matter."
> **Natalie Saranga Omattage:** *Intel Foundation Young Scientist, Intel International Science and Engineering Fair; Semifinalist, Siemens Competition; University of Richmond Class of 2012*

Since the paper is so important to the Siemens Competition, you should consult Chapter 12 on how to write a publishable paper. Amanda Mason, who made it to the regional finals, suggests soliciting the help of a qualified mentor.

> "This goes for all the competitions: Find an adviser who can help you write the abstract and paper you will submit! It's important to have someone who is a Ph.D. in some part of biology if you do biology, chemistry if you do chemistry, etc. It doesn't really need to be more specific than that. If you work at a lab at a university, your lab mentor may be able to help; but if he/she is too busy, someone who teaches science is a great choice. Your adviser will help you write a good paper, because no matter how intelligent you are and no matter how many other papers you have read, you won't know how to write a good paper nearly as well as a Ph.D. will."
> **Amanda R. Mason:** *Regional Finalist, Siemens Competition; Regional Finalist, Junior Science and Humanities Symposium; Harvard Class of 2009*

When writing the paper, it is necessary to emphasize its importance, especially how it will impact society.

> "Your paper needs to be dynamite to make it to regionals; start the paper months ahead of time."
> **Maria Elena de Obaldia:** *Best of Category in Microbiology, Intel International Science and Engineering Fair; Regional Finalist, Siemens Competition; Harvard Class of 2008*

In addition to one original and three hard copies of your report, the abstract, research report and references must be saved onto a CD and mailed in with your paper copies. After the initial review, up to 300 projects will be selected as semifinalists. Each semifinalist receives a Siemens Competition backpack with goodies such as an iPod Shuffle or digital picture frame.

Second Phase: Regional Finals

Among the 300 semifinalists, up to 30 individual students and 30 teams are selected as regional finalists. In early November, the regional finalists will compete at six regional competitions hosted by various universities including MIT, Carnegie Mellon, Georgia Tech, Notre Dame, UT Austin and California Institute of Technology. Regional finalists will spend three days at the regional competition, during which they will present to a panel of judges from the host university. In addition to a poster presentation, finalists must also deliver a 12-minute oral presentation followed by a question-and-answer session.

> "At Siemens, presentation counts. Both a poster presentation and a slide presentation are required. Also, the panel of judges, which may include a few Nobel laureates, will drill you at the question session to make sure you truly know your field. Be prepared to defend your project and show the judges problem solving skills when they ask you general questions."
> **Philip Mocz:** *Eighth Place, Intel Science Talent Search; Second Place Team, Siemens Competition; Finalist, Intel International Science and Engineering Fair; Finalist, Junior Science and Humanities Symposium; Harvard Class of 2012*

> "It's important to have a great paper in order to be selected as a regional finalist; once you get there, though, it's all about the presentation. You have to be passionate about your research in order to impress these judges. In addition, Siemens brings in very high caliber judges who were fairly intimidating during the question sessions; I really had to defend my research and even my hypothesis against questions they brought up. I recommend being confident with the logic behind your project and having a comprehensive understanding of your area of research—even of things only tangentially related to your project—judges look for depth as well as breadth of knowledge."
> **Alicia Darnell:** *Second Place, Siemens Competition; Best of Category in Medicine and Health, Intel International Science and Engineering Fair; National Finalist, Junior Science and Humanities Symposium; Yale Class of 2012*

Winners of the regional competition receive a silver medal and scholarships of $3,000 for individual projects and $6,000 for team projects, which will be divided among the members. Only the regional winners will advance as national finalists. Each finalist will receive a bronze medal and a $1,000 scholarship. Each regional finalist's high school also receives $2,000 to fund and support science, mathematics and technology programs. In addition to the prestige, recognition and privilege of presenting their projects to distinguished scientists, finalists will receive the Siemens Competition backpack and associated goodies.

In addition to the competition, there is also an open house at each of the regional competitions. Professional scientists, college admissions officers, Siemens Competition alumni, high school students and the public are welcomed to view the projects.

Third Phase: National Finals

Congratulations on making it this far! By being selected among thousands of applicants, you are recognized by the Siemens Competition as one of the top high school researchers in the country. At the national finals, you will be competing against the winners of the regional competitions: six individuals and six teams. The national competition is a week-long event in early December that takes place in New York City. The judging at national finals is similar to the judging at the regional finals.

> "Remember when I said not to do something because your mentor told you so, and always to ask questions? Siemens is a big reason why. Make sure you know the interesting points of your project and the questions the project raises, and be able to answer them to the best of your knowledge! If you're a Siemens regional/national finalist, have an hour (at least) chat with your mentor over your paper and PowerPoint, ask him/her what questions it brings up and see if you can answer them and also use the time to bring up any questions you might have. The judging is tough."
>
> **Adam Solomon:** *Third Place, Siemens Competition; Eighth Place, Intel Science Talent Search; Yale Class of 2010*

The judges at the national levels will be extremely familiar with your project. They want to know that your knowledge is thorough and that you are passionate about your research. Although the presentation is important in showing how well you know your project, the question-and-answer session is probably the most important factor in determining the winners.

> "Make the most of the Q&A session with the judges. This is your time to show that you're not just a pretty package, but that you actually know what you did and why you did what you did."
>
> **Yin Li:** *First Place, Siemens Competition; Finalist, Intel International Science and Engineering Fair; Harvard Class of 2008*

> "The competition here is very difficult but be confident in your work and don't be too discouraged if you don't do as well as you'd like. The judges here are looking for very professional presentations so stay away from gimmicks that may impress a general audience but may not have a lot of scientific expertise. Also, if you get a difficult question don't be afraid to say that you don't know the answer. That is better than making up an answer."
>
> **Arun Thottumkara:** *Second Place, Siemens Competition; First Place, National Junior Science and Humanities Symposium; Semifinalist, Intel Science Talent Search; Best of Category in Chemistry, Intel International Science and Engineering Fair; Harvard Class of 2008*

Once the judging sessions are over, there is a National Recognition Gala Dinner in New York City on that Sunday. Competition winners will be announced at a press conference on Monday. As national finalists, each student or team will receive a gold medal and scholarships ranging from $10,000 (sixth place) to $100,000 (first place). Another benefit of making it to the national finals of the Siemens Competition is that the finalists are invited to ring the closing bell at the New York Stock Exchange. (How many times will you ever get to do something like that, especially as a high school student?)

The Siemens Competition is a prestigious and rewarding high school science research competition that focuses initially on the quality of the paper and subsequently on the presentation. The Siemens Competition consists of three stages: semifinals, regional finals and national finals. Although the competition is a rigorous and stressful process, the friendships and connections that you make at the competitions will last a lifetime.

"The best part of participating in high school science competitions is the opportunity to meet others who have similar interests. As a result, I most strongly recommend that participants get to know other participants. For example, at the national finals of the Siemens Competition, we were given an entire day just for social time. I am still in contact with many of the people I met during the competition and I will almost certainly see some again in college."
Hayden Metsky: *Sixth Place, Siemens Competition; Finalist, Intel Science Talent Search; Finalist, Intel International Science and Engineering Fair*

"Siemens is a contest that treats you like royalty. All of the people who organize the Siemens Competition are enthusiastic about your work. They send a car to pick you up at the airport and then you spend several days in a fancy hotel eating good food. At the national competition they took us to see Mary Poppins on Broadway and treated us to nice dinners out. They shower you with stuff—I got a camera, an iPod, tons of notebooks and pencils from colleges, several tee-shirts, chocolate, an umbrella—you name it. When my teammate and I arrived in New York we walked into our hotel rooms to find bags filled with candy. Siemens is a competition that likes their students.

Siemens also gets a huge amount of publicity. There are reporters at the awards ceremonies at both the regional and national level. As a finalist, you get media training because you will be interviewed at one point or another. My partner and I had several interviews in connection with Siemens. We even had one about an hour after the national awards ceremony—the kind where our reporter back home talked to us through ear pieces while we looked at the camera. The presentation style for Siemens matches the focus on media. You need to have a polished, professional 12-minute PowerPoint talk for both judges and an audience followed by a 12-minute Q&A session with the judges alone. The judges have already read your report and you have a full 24 minutes to impress them, so deep, complicated projects can do very well at Siemens."
Erika Alden DeBenedictis: *Davidson Fellow; First Place, Intel Science Talent Search; Best of Category in Team, Intel International Science and Engineering Fair; Third Place Team, Siemens Competition; Caltech Class of 2014*

Take-Home Points

- You need to be a high school senior to enter an individual project. If you are not yet a senior you can still enter as part of a team.
- Your paper is the most important factor in qualifying for the regional finals.
- Practice, practice, practice your presentation in front of your mentors and others.
- You will be judged by high caliber scientists so be prepared.
- Show your breadth and depth of knowledge.
- Have fun! Make lots of friends because you might see them again in college.

To learn more about an individual's experience during the competition, visit Benjamin Pollack's blog at:

http://www.sciencebuddies.org/science-fair projects/blog_benjamin_pollack_siemens.shtml

Other useful links:

http://www.siemens-foundation.org/en/competition.htm
http://www.collegeboard.com/siemens/index.html

18

Intel Science Talent Search

A scientist in his laboratory is not a mere technician: he is also a child confronting
natural phenomena that impress him as though they were fairy tales.
Marie Curie

East of Oklahoma

Mary Masterman is a scientific force to be reckoned with—do not let her
love of birds and fluency in multiple languages fool you. Originally from
Oklahoma City, Mary used her curiosity for the natural world to propel herself
onto the national stage. At 17 Mary built a Littrow spectrograph system—
which normally costs around $20,000-$100,000—for only $300. Despite its
inexpensive construction, Mary's spectrograph made accurate measurements
comparable to published data. Although she won many awards for this
achievement, Mary's crowning scientific award was first place at the Intel
Science Talent Search (STS), which entailed a $100,000 college scholarship that
has enabled her to attend the Massachusetts Institute of Technology.

What is the Intel Science Talent Search?

Also sometimes colloquially known as the "Junior Nobel Prize," Intel STS is
a science research competition that catapults 40 of America's brightest and
most talented young scientists onto the national stage. Originally founded by
Westinghouse Electric Corporation in 1942, the Science Talent Search was ad-
opted by Intel and the Society for Science and the Public in 1998 and holds the
title of "America's oldest and most prestigious science research competition
for high school seniors."

By the end of January, 300 students from around the nation are selected
as semifinalists. Each of the 300 semifinalists receives a $1,000 scholarship.
The semifinalists are then whittled down to 40 finalists. In the middle of

March, 40 finalists from across the nation, selected from a pool of thousands of students, spend a week in Washington, D.C., at the Science Talent Institute. Each of the 40 finalists receives a $7,500 scholarship and a laptop computer. In addition to competing for the grand award of $100,000, the finalists present their projects to prominent scientists at the National Academy of Sciences, undergo rigorous judging sessions and meet with distinguished government leaders. The Intel Science Talent Search not only judges the merit of your research project, but also tests your scientific knowledge and thought-processes.

Application Process

The Intel Science Talent Search requires an extensive application that is similar to a college application. The application is comprised of a questionnaire requesting information about your academic achievements, recommendation letters from your mentor and science teachers, a detailed report describing your research and essays responding to a number or prompts. The application is typically due in the middle of November. The eligibility requirements for STS are similar to those for International Science and Engineering Fair (ISEF), except for the following:

• Only high school seniors are eligible to apply to STS.
• STS applicants must have completed their high school graduation requirements.
• Team projects are ineligible for STS.
Projects involving live non-human vertebrate animal experimentation are ineligible for STS.

Starting from the year 2011, the Intel Science Talent Search will be switching from paper submissions to an online entry system. Most of the application, with the exception of official student transcripts, will be uploaded through this online system. (Transcripts will only be accepted in paper copy and in a sealed envelope signed by a counselor or administrator.) However, the content of the new application will primarily remain the same as previous years, so the advice provided in the Guide will still be applicable.

Intel STS maintains especially strong academic integrity and ethical standards. In particular, the new STS application process prohibits mentors (or other adults) from compensating their students for competition performance.

The information provided in this *Guide* section follows the organization of the STS application; hence, it should be read in parallel with the actual application if possible.

The Research Report

For the Intel Science Talent Search, the research report is one of the most important aspects of the application. It cannot exceed 20 pages, including text and all appendices, tables, and charts. The bibliography does not count towards the page limit. During the initial rounds of judging, the report is read by multiple experts in your field. Also, the judges at the finals thoroughly read the report weeks in advance to fully understand your project and to test your understanding. In addition to the report, you must also include a 100-word summary of the project in layperson's terms and a 250-word scientific abstract. The summary will be used primarily for press-release purposes, especially if you are selected as a finalist.

> "Spend a lot of time writing your research paper. Emphasize how your project will impact society and why it is important. Spend a lot of time on the essays, too. The judges are looking for students who are serious about having a career in science or engineering, so you should focus on why you enjoy science and your past experiences that relate to science and engineering. At the same time, you want to show them you have other interests, too."
> **Amber Hess:** *First Place in Chemistry, Intel International Science and Engineering Fair; Finalist, Intel Science Talent Search; Semifinalist, Siemens Competition; MIT Class of 2009.*

> "Start writing the paper as soon as possible. Have your mentor and other research scientists proofread it. Time spent on paper and application should be comparable with time spent on the experiments themselves."
> **Dayan Li:** *Intel Foundation Young Scientist, Intel International Science and Engineering Fair; Semifinalist, Intel Science Talent Search; Harvard Class of 2011*

> "In terms of the application, the most important thing is to start early. This way you can include your entire personality and individuality and also edit your work several times."
> **Lauren R. Lisann:** *Finalist, Intel Science Talent Search; Semifinalist, Siemens Competition; Winner, American Academy of Neurology Neuroscience Research Prize; Yale Class of 2012*

Part I: Student Entry Form

The first part of the application is the student questionnaire. This component of the application should be treated like a college application. A separate résumé that contains additional information about your achievements may be added.

The entry form requires that you choose a category for your project. The category choice determines which experts will be reading your research report, so it would be in your best interest to choose the category that most closely matches your project.

Another important question in the application form asks for the most influential person in the development of your scientific career. Choose this person wisely! If you advance to the final round of STS, a special surprise for both of you will be revealed.

Part II: Essay Questions

Essay Questions 1-4
Since the essay questions are a significant portion of the application, these

are extremely important. You should allocate sufficient time to complete them and aim to personalize them as much as possible. Focus on why you enjoy science and what past experiences you have that relate to science and engineering. The judges are looking for students who are serious about pursuing careers in science or engineering. Unlike other competitions, STS wants to assess your breadth of scientific knowledge, not just your knowledge of your own field. They want to know that you are passionate about science, but it is advisable to show that you have other interests as well.

> "In your essays, describe the passion you have for your research and your field and show that your scientific inquiry stems from a love for, and innate questioning of, science/math, not just a college résumé addition."
> **Alexis Mychajliw:** *Finalist, Intel Science Talent Search; Cornell Class of 2012*

Essay Questions 5 (a-f)
In this section, you should illustrate the kind of research experience you have had. Your explanation should be supported by the supervising scientist form.

Part IIA, Part III: Supervising Scientist Form and Recommendation Letters
The supervising scientists form for part IIA should be written by your principal investigator or mentor. By the time of submission, you should have developed a strong relationship with your mentor so that he or she can vouch for your scientific talent and great potential for a successful scientific career (see Chapter 9). The recommendation letter for Part III should be from a teacher, advisor, guidance counselor or mentor from your high school. As with other recommendation letters, give them notice long before the deadline.

Part IV: Secondary School Record
This section is straightforward—it just asks for records of your high school studies. But remember to make sure that your high school principal, rather than your guidance counselor, signs the form.

Sending in the Application
It is important to follow the application directions. Keeping track of all the components of the application can be overwhelming, so pay attention to instructions. Do not leave submission to the last minute.

Congratulations You Are a Finalist! What Next?
If you are selected as a finalist, you will be notified before the finalist results are scheduled to be announced publicly.

In terms of short-term preparation before the competition, there is not much else you can do other than review your science notes and practice presenting your project. Not only will the judges at STS test your understanding of your field of interest, they will also test your general knowledge and understanding of other major scientific disciplines. Although it may be difficult, it would be worthwhile to read papers from fields other than your own. You do not need to understand everything in these papers, but if you can follow the thought process you are in good shape. In addition, you can read popular scientific literature such as *Discover* or articles on *www.howstuffworks.com* to get a broad idea about other scientific disciplines.

> "Step out of your comfort zone and read about quantum mechanics if you're a cell biologist, and vice versa. It is not necessarily about memorizing any specific fact; it is about stimulating your thought process in areas that you've never considered before."
> **Alexis Mychajliw:** *Finalist, Intel Science Talent Search; Cornell Class of 2012*

Throughout the week of competition, usually from March 11-17, you will be busy from around 7 a.m. to 9 p.m., so try your best to get some sleep. There will be presentations, media sessions, speakers and dinners with the distinguished judges. Since you will be associating with judges and other important people affiliated with Intel and the Society for Science and the Public, it is important to be on your best behavior. Try to engage in interesting and memorable discussions. You will have rounds of rigorous judging sessions and a chance to present your project at the National Academy of Sciences. Despite the busy schedule, one of the most important aspects of STS is making friends with your fellow student scientists. Some of the friends you make at STS may be among your closest and you will probably keep in touch throughout college and beyond. Try not to have an overly competitive attitude towards your fellow finalists. They are your best resources—and they may be your future collaborators.

> "After a judging round, all of us would work together to solve the impossible math problem or teach each other the basics of chemical solubility laws. The conversation you have with the physicist next to you could give you the edge when your astronomy judge arrives."
> **Alexis Mychajliw:** *Finalist, Intel Science Talent Search; Cornell Class of 2012*

> "This is the competition where not only your knowledge of your project counts, but an understanding in all the major fields of science is expected. Before the competition, the judges have actually spent weeks reviewing each of the finalists' projects and they know them well. Be prepared to be challenged by all sorts of intriguing and tough science, science history and science policy questions. Also, this competition is an opportunity to form a strong network with the other finalists."
> **Philip Mocz:** *Eighth Place, Intel Science Talent Search; Second Place Team, Siemens Competition; Finalist, Intel International Science and Engineering Fair; Finalist, Junior Science and Humanities Symposium; Harvard Class of 2012*

Judging Sessions

Intel STS judging sessions are unique and difficult to prepare for. During each session, there are approximately four judges sitting at the table across from you, a situation similar to some job interviews. The judges test your scientific knowledge and your ability to think critically. They may also ask about science policy and history. Many times they will try to derive the questions from your application. For example, if you are a violin player, they may ask you the properties of sound waves. Here are more sample questions:

1. Are there silicon based life forms?
2. How do the tides work?
3. If you were the director of national energy policy, what would your energy policy be?

If you get completely stumped on a question, do not give up. Try to reason your way through the answer out loud. Even if your answer is wrong, you may get points for an interesting thought process. Do not freak out; relax and have fun. Do not be afraid to ask questions of the judges; if used appropriately, these questions may help clarify the prompt or give you some more time to think it through.

> "Just relax and tell the judges what you do know. Don't be afraid to ask questions and propose solutions to problems even if you are unsure of the answer. The judges really want to see your scientific thought process."
> **Meredith MacGregor:** *Intel Foundation Young Scientist, Intel International Science and Engineering Fair; Ninth Place, Intel Science Talent Search; Harvard Class of 2011*

> "There is no real way to "cram" or prepare for it aside from practicing your presentation and knowing as much as possible about the field in which you performed your research. The judging sessions are meant to test your overall knowledge of math and science outside your area of research, as well as your ability to think critically. It is therefore difficult to predict just what the judges will ask."
> **Lauren R. Lisann:** *Finalist, Intel Science Talent Search; Semifinalist, Siemens Competition; Winner, American Academy of Neurology Neuroscience Research Prize; Yale Class of 2012*

> "Once you make it to the top 40, STS is a lot different from ISEF in that, although much of the competition involves a poster competition, the rest involves being interviewed by judges on a one-by-one basis about your overall knowledge of science in general. For that part of STS, I would suggest, as early as you can, really getting into science and asking questions about everything—reading science magazines, surfing Wikipedia to learn about things, etc. That can give you the competitive edge. They tend to ask you very in-depth questions about your category and your project, so it is helpful, a few days before, to go back and review everything. For instance, before I was judged, I went back and researched some details of infrared and other types of spectroscopy that I did not completely remember. It did not directly relate to my project, but the judges ended up asking me several questions about infrared spectroscopy, and I did much better than I would have if I hadn't done the research."
> **Mary Masterman:** *First Place, Intel Science Talent Search; Best of Category in Physics, Intel International Science and Engineering Fair; Research Science Institute; MIT Class of 2011*

> "Besides knowing enough to write a 20-page research paper, you have to be able to apply AP-level physics, math, chemistry and biology. The Intel STS competition is pretty standard in the semifinalist round (submitting a 20-page research paper with

a couple of good teacher recommendations), but gets quite hairy in the finals. The judging interviews in the final round are the toughest I've ever seen in a competition and are focused on your general math and science background, which seems to be weighted equally with your research project. A lot of the questions ask you to explain phenomena with your math, physics, chemistry or biology knowledge and can be really tricky, taking much more time than the interview to solve. Luckily, the judges give partial credit if you tell them the answer during the next interview, the next day or even over dinner.

"Hands down, the best part about STS is the people. The students who you get the privilege of meeting are ridiculously brilliant and will be your future classmates at various Ivy League schools. A close second is the first-class treatment, including receiving tons of publicity, getting a lot of free stuff (including giant novelty checks), staying at the St. Regis Hotel and meeting the President."

Michael Loy: *Inductee, National Gallery for America's Young Inventors; Finalist, Intel Science Talent Search; Second Place in Engineering, Intel International Science and Engineering Fair; Harvey Mudd College Class of 2013*

Presenting at the National Academy of Sciences

The National Academy of Sciences (NAS) is a society of distinguished scholars engaged in scientific and engineering research, dedicated to the advancement of science and technology. The NAS was established by President Abraham Lincoln at the height of the Civil War. Since then, the nation's leaders have turned to the NAS, which includes 2,100 members and nearly 200 Nobel Prize laureates, for advice on scientific and technological issues.

At the NAS, you will have the honor and privilege to present your project to judges and the public. Before arriving in Washington, D.C., you should have practiced your presentation, reviewed your report and brushed up on important literature. During this session, judges will come by your project to ask questions and test how much you know about your project. In a later session, the public will be allowed to enter, but you may also be judged during this time, so stay on guard.

"The judges not only want you to be fluent in scientific jargon, they also want you to be able to present your project to any person who enters the NAS, child or adult. I gathered a crowd of young kids by talking to them about what they enjoyed: bugs. As soon as I caught their attention with my eccentric project I did not necessarily present my thesis; rather, I let them ask me questions about whatever interested them and never lost my patience. The judges at my presentation were far more concerned with asking me random questions about dragonflies and how I would apply my research, rather than the logistics of the research itself. Learn about your field and contemporary issues, because in the end they just want to see that you love what you do."

Alexis Mychajliw: *Finalist, Intel Science Talent Search; Cornell Class of 2012*

The judges may ask seemingly random questions that do not exactly relate to your project, but may have relevance in your field. It would be wise to read up on the latest research, which would show how passionate you are and how much you enjoy your subject.

The judges will "look for ownership of the project and for the creativity and ingenuity of the individual student that cannot be replaced by the hand of a friendly professor."
Alexis Mychajliw: *Finalist, Intel Science Talent Search; Cornell Class of 2012*

The Intel Science Talent Search may be one of the most memorable and possibly life-changing science competitions you will participate in. The friendships you develop over sharing lab experiences and other activities will last a lifetime. Make the most of your week there by interacting with the other finalists and by simply having fun. Even if you do not place in the top ten, you might still receive the Glen T. Seaborg award: essentially "the most social" of the finalists. This is presented at the end of the week, when the finalists vote for the one person they feel would be the best representative of their STS class to speak during the awards ceremony. Although this does not entail a monetary award, it is truly a high honor.

"If you make it to finalist and are invited to the gathering in D.C., remember to enjoy yourself. You've already won the competition and meeting people is just as important as deciding the relative rankings."
Greg Brockman: *Sixth Place, Intel Science Talent Search; Semifinalist, Siemens Competition; Finalist, Junior Science and Humanities Symposium; Harvard Class of 2011*

It may help to keep a journal during the week, to record your memories and thoughts throughout the day. If you feel stressed during the judging sessions, remember that you have already been recognized by STS as one of the top 40 high school scientists in the nation! Reaching this point is already an amazing accomplishment. You never know what the judges are thinking, so do not give up.

In Their Words

"The application is the hardest part of STS because of the sheer number of people you're competing against. Through your essays, show that you are a focused and intelligent science student, not just a smart person. The best essays I've seen brought together and discussed independent research and thinking in many fields, including hobbies, to show why and how a person has an exceptional scientific mind. Think of it as a college application for science—which is basically what the application process is.

"The judging at STS is very hard to prepare for because of the variety of questions, the length of judging and the lack of (public) rubrics or criteria for the process. The best advice, though, is simply to be yourself and think out loud. You'll be asked questions about everything from advanced mathematics to archeology, from astrophysics to modern art, and you will be asked plenty of questions that you have no idea how to answer—the judging is absolutely designed to stump you. As such, answering questions correctly isn't as important as showing the judges that you can think quickly and clearly during your 15-minute judging period (though being right never hurts either). Talk to your judges outside of scheduled judging time, also — this is the only science fair I know of where you eat dinner with the people who are "controlling your fate," and they really are interested in getting to know you as a person instead of just as the mind behind a science project.

On public viewing day, reach out to the students who visit; they come to the National Academy to see what the "best and brightest" are doing. Also, don't be afraid to talk to the many TV crews, who are there to watch science in action. Start conversations with reporters, with students and with all the staff who are there to help you; they all love to talk to students who are doing amazing science. It has benefits for you as well; one of my friends impressed the judges by giving an incredibly clear description of crystal resonance and why it was important—to an 8-year-old.

And, if you're a finalist, spend as much time as you possibly can with the other 39. They are some of the most brilliant, amazing people you'll meet, and chances are you'll go to college with a fair number of them!"

Stephen Trusheim: *First Place, sanofi-aventis BioGENEius Challenge; Finalist, Intel Science Talent Search; First Place in Category, Intel International Science and Engineering Fair; Finalist, National Junior Science and Humanities Symposium; Regional Finalist, Young Epidemiology Scholars Competition; Semifinalist, Siemens Competition; Stanford Class of 2013*

"Going to Washington, D.C., to compete for one of the top ten winners' spots was an incredible and unforgettable experience. The competition features a rigorous panel-style judging that takes place to test finalists' scientific knowledge and challenge their ability to solve problems. What was most surprising to me was the balance struck between judging my project and judging my scientific thinking abilities. To be successful in both aspects, it's important to think out loud, to try an answer even if you're fairly sure it's the wrong one. Recently, I found out that these types of tricky questions are also used in many job interviews for finance positions, so the experience of being made to think on your feet and consider aspects of a subject that you never did before is definitely a valuable one. Intel STS also creates a parent- and advisor-free environment that enables students to evolve from competitors to acquaintances and friends. There is a lot of free time allotted for bonding over more than projects, and over the course of the week in Washington, I made friends with whom I still keep in touch and even lunch with at school! My advice for the Intel STS is to spend time with the other 134 finalists; there's a good chance you might go to college together!

"Even though it's a stressful experience to answer the chemistry, biology or physics questions of notable scientists, my best advice is to enjoy the time you're given there. The week is filled with amazing activities, such as meeting President Obama, dining with Intel scientists and even getting a minor planet named after me! The entire week made me proud of the work I accomplished; the awards ceremony at the end is beautiful and the entire week instilled me with the message that even as a student, I have the power to accomplish great things. Intel STS inspired me to continue pursuing research, to have confidence in my potential and reminded me of the importance of science in the community."

Chelsea Lynn Jurman: *Fifth Place, Intel Science Talent Search; Third Place, Young Epidemiology Scholars Competition; Yale Class of 2013*

Take-Home Points

- Only high school seniors can apply.
- The initial judging process looks at your research project, academic scores, essays and recommendation letters.
- At the finalist level, you will be judged on your knowledge of general science concepts and logical thinking skills.

If you would like a detailed look at what Intel STS is like, please visit these blogs:

Amber's 2005 Intel Science Talent Search Blog
http://www.sciencebuddies.org/science-fair-projects/blog_amber_hess_sts.shtml

Mr. Solomon Goes to Washington
http://stsfinals.blogspot.com/

Intel Science Talent Search
http://www.societyforscience.org/sts

19

Other Major Competitions

There are two possible outcomes: if the result confirms the hypothesis, then you've made a discovery. If the result is contrary to the hypothesis, then you've made a discovery.
Enrico Fermi

Although ISEF, Siemens and STS are prestigious and fun to compete in, unfortunately not everyone can enter these competitions. What if you do not have a regional ISEF affiliated fair near you? What if you are not yet a senior? What if you cannot develop a team project? Don't worry! There are a number of other well-known competitions for secondary school researchers. These include the Davidson Fellowship, Junior Science and Humanities Symposium, Junior Academy of Sciences, Young Epidemiology Scholars Competition, sanofi-aventis BioGENEius Challenge and National Gallery for America's Young Inventors. In this chapter, previous winners of these competitions will offer advice and describe the process of each competition.

Davidson Fellowship
The Davidson Fellowship is awarded by the Davidson Institute for Talent Development, whose mission is "to recognize, nurture and support profoundly intelligent young people and to provide opportunities for them to develop their talents to make a positive difference." You may have first heard about the Davidson Institute in elementary school; they are known for their widely successful "Math Blaster™" and "Reading Blaster™" computer series. The goal of the Davidson Fellows scholarship is to recognize extremely intelligent students under the age of 18 for significant pieces of work that have the potential to positively impact society. Although there are many categories in which to enter, including science, technology, mathematics, music, literature, philosophy and any other graduate-level work that is considered

"out-of-the-box," a significant number of the award recipients are involved in scientific research. Each fellow receives an award of $50,000, $25,000 or $10,000. In addition to the monetary award, the Davidson Fellows are honored in Washington, D.C., with Congressional meetings and a reception.

> "You also get to meet other students who have done significant work—and not just in science! I met piano prodigies, a philosopher and a couple writers. I've kept in contact with several of the students I met, all of whom are fascinating people. During your stay in D.C. you also have the opportunity to meet one or two of your state's senators or representatives. Being a Davidson Fellow exposes you to a collection of exciting new people and experiences."
> **Erika Alden DeBenedictis:** *Davidson Fellow; First Place, Intel Science Talent Search; Best of Category in Team, Intel International Science and Engineering Fair; Third Place Team, Siemens Competition; Caltech Class of 2014*

The Davidson Fellows Application, due the first Wednesday in March every year, is comprised of all required elements of your work, three different nomination forms and a 15-minute DVD about you and your work. The judging criteria include the scope and quality of the work, level of significance of the work and the applicant's depth of knowledge and understanding of the work.

> "Unlike many of the other science competitions, the Davidson Fellow scholarships are awarded entirely on your application. Additionally, the Davidson Fellow scholarship is open to all academic fields of study and all types of art. The application process for this competition is relatively long in comparison to many of the other science research competitions, complete with multiple essays and a recorded self-interview. I tried to write the essays without including too much scientific jargon, while still getting across the general concept. Most importantly, however, I continually emphasized the impact that my research can have on society and the world at large. The Davidson Scholarship is generally geared toward projects that will have some real-world impact. For the recorded self-interview, I gave a short presentation and explanation of my project, using the PowerPoint I made for JSHS as an outline."
> **Nolan Kamitaki:** *Davidson Fellow; Second Place in Medicine and Health, Intel International Science and Engineering Fair; Semifinalist, Intel Science Talent Search; Semifinalist, Young Epidemiology Scholars Competition; Finalist, Junior Science and Humanities Symposium; Waiakea High School Class of 2010*

> "If you're thinking about applying for a Davidson Fellowship, then you need to start NOW. First you need to check to make sure you will be under 18 at the awards ceremony in the fall. Then you start on the most extensive application you will probably ever attempt. For research projects you submit the usual report and abstract. Then you also submit long essays about the significance of your project, your project's benefit to society, your project's possible applications, how you did your project, how you got the idea, and who helped you. You also submit a video and a 'computer model'- basically a CD with whatever you want on it. I submitted a 12-minute video and a CD with my computer program and a website. Then you ask a mentor, a teacher and a professional in the field to submit extensive references about you and your project. It sounds like a lot of work and I was daunted at first, but it actually helped me clarify my thoughts on my project.

The only things you don't need to submit are a transcript or test scores from your school. This is because the Davidson Institute sees your work as all the proof they need that you're an amazing kid. When you send your application away, it doesn't go into a black hole—it goes to real people who read it and think about it. When I got to D.C. I found out that all the people there already knew my name and what my project was. You get to meet Mr. and Mrs. Davidson, who run the whole show, and you get the sense that they really care about your future. They tell you to keep them posted about how you're doing. Being a Davidson Fellow is an experience not just because of the recognition and the scholarship, but also because of the Davidsons' continued interest in your career."

Erika Alden DeBenedictis: *Davidson Fellow; First Place, Intel Science Talent Search; Best of Category in Team, Intel International Science and Engineering Fair; Third Place Team, Siemens Competition; Caltech Class of 2014*

"The Davidson Fellowship is a really comprehensive competition. The long list of required items for the application (PowerPoint, DVD, research paper, etc.) may seem discouraging, but I found that, as reluctant as I was at first to film myself talking about my research, that and the other parts of the application process helped me to refine my presentation skills and really put together a thoughtful description of what I had done. What is the point of doing great work if you cannot communicate it effectively? The Davidson Fellowship emphasized the importance of communication and presentation. In addition, the couple of days spent in Washington, D.C., with the other fellows were a great experience. Although a good number of the Davidson Fellows had done science projects, there were fellows with expertise in music, literature and social studies as well, and it was interesting to hear about their work. It was also amazing to meet my congressional representatives and talk with them about my work and about their perspectives on science research and education."

Fiona Wood: *Davidson Fellow; Second Place in Category, Intel International Science and Engineering Fair; Harvard Class of 2013*

Although the Davidson Institute acknowledges that it is looking for "extraordinary" applicants, do not be intimidated. Chances are high that you fall into that category! You should apply, even if filming a DVD about yourself feels a little uncomfortable. For more information about the competition and the extensive application process, please visit: *http://www.davidsongifted.org/fellows/*

Junior Science and Humanities Symposia (JSHS)

The Junior Science and Humanities Symposia (JSHS), endorsed by the National Association of Secondary School Principals (NASSP), holds regional and national symposia in 48 regions.

In order to compete in JSHS, you must enter through a regional symposium near your home. You must submit a written report, which will be reviewed by a panel of judges. Once you submit your paper, you will be notified whether your project is eligible to enter the competition. At the regional symposium, each presenter has 12 minutes to present a slide presentation followed by a six-minute question-and-answer period. Previous JSHS participants stress the importance of a stellar slide presentation.

"Be confident in your work and don't be too discouraged if you don't do as well as you'd like. The judges here are looking for very professional presentations, so stay away from gimmicks that may impress a general audience but not one that has a lot of scientific expertise. Also, if you get a difficult question, don't be afraid to say that you don't know the answer. That is better than making up an answer."

Arun Thottumkara: *Second Place, Siemens Competition; First Place, National Junior Science and Humanities Symposium; Semifinalist, Intel Science Talent Search; Best of Category in Chemistry, Intel International Science and Engineering Fair; Harvard Class of 2008*

"My impression of this competition was that the presentation was just as important, if not more, than the actual science. In other words, your project wasn't judged for its potential applications to science, but instead it was judged on how you presented it. Make sure your PowerPoint is aesthetically pleasing, detailed and logical for this competition. The judges are less specifically selected, also, so make sure you give sufficient background information and explain your research on a comprehensible level."

Alicia Darnell: *Second Place, Siemens Competition; Best of Category in Medicine and Health, Intel International Science and Engineering Fair; Finalist, National Junior Science and Humanities Symposium; Yale Class of 2012*

Even if your slide presentation does not go well, do not be discouraged. There could also be a problem on the side of the judges. A common problem that presenters face in this competition is that the judges may be unfamiliar with the subject area, whereas judges at ISEF, Siemens and Intel STS are selected specifically from your field.

"Applied science is highly valued at this competition. Everything is determined by one PowerPoint presentation followed by a question-and-answer session. Defend your project well and give focused responses. Listen to the presentation of the other students. It is amazing to learn what others your age are doing."

Philip Mocz: *Eighth Place, Intel Science Talent Search; Second Place Team, Siemens Competition; Finalist, Intel International Science and Engineering Fair; Finalist, National Junior Science and Humanities Symposium; Harvard Class of 2012*

At each regional symposium, five finalists are selected to go on an expense-paid trip to the national JSHS. However, only the first- and second-place finalists at each regional symposium are allowed to present their research at nationals. The top three regional finalists are awarded $2,000, $1,500 and $1,000 respectively. At nationals, six first-place awardees (each in a different category) each receive $12,000, six second-place awardees each receive $8,000 and six third-place awardees each receive $4,000. In addition, each of the first-place winners at nationals earns an expense-paid trip to the London International Youth Science Forum where 400 participants from 60 nations present their research.

In any case, if you feel that your project has many applications and you are good at presenting, you should definitely enter this competition. For more information visit: *http://www.jshs.org/*.

American Junior Academy of Science (AJAS)

If you are looking for a competition that focuses more on students' research rather than competition itself, then the American Junior Academy of Sciences (AJAS) is just for you. The American Junior Academy of Sciences is affiliated with the American Association for the Advancement of Science (AAAS). Every year, AJAS delegates from across the country attend the national AAAS conference and present their research alongside professional research scientists. In order to attend the national conference, delegates are selected from 44 affiliated state junior academies of sciences and are judged based on the quality of their research projects. Once selected as a delegate, the student will be inducted as an AJAS Fellow and is affiliated with the National Association of Academies of Science (NAAS). The national AJAS events are noncompetitive.

> "Would the Nobel laureates compete to see who is the 'champion' or the best? While there are many national science competitions, AJAS is the only national honor society that not only profiles young scientific achievement, but exposes them to the best science in the world at AAAS (the American Association for the Advancement of Science), publisher of *Science* magazine."
> **Joan M. Messer:** *Co-Director, American Junior Academy of Science*

Once the students are chosen by the state academies to attend AJAS, they are also eligible to apply to attend other events such as the International Science and Engineering Camp (ISEC) and the Korean Science Festival. These are great, noncompetitive programs that help foster a network of student researchers who are passionate about science. For more information, visit: *http://www.amjas.org.*

Young Epidemiology Scholars (YES) Competition

YES! Are you excited about epidemiology? Have you ever wondered how the aftermath of a natural disaster affects the health of a population, or how the bird flu might impact the world? If so, you should consider entering the Young Epidemiology Scholars (YES) Competition. Sponsored by the Robert Wood Johnson Foundation and administered by the College Board, this nationwide scholarship competition allows students to submit original research projects that explore ways to improve the health of the public by applying methods used in epidemiology. The deadline to register your project is the first of February—do not miss it, because there are many chances to win awards. Up to 120 students receive college scholarships ranging from $1,000 to $50,000. Of these, up to 60 semifinalists receive awards of $1,000, and up to 60 regional finalists receive an expense-paid trip to compete in the regional and national competitions in April in Washington, D.C. Of those regional finalists, 48 will receive scholarship awards of $2,000. The other 12 will compete in the national finals where six will receive $15,000, two will receive $20,000, another two will receive $35,000. The top two national winners will receive $50,000 each. In addition to many opportunities to win scholarships, YES Competition participants will have a chance to meet other students interested in epidemiology, and they will also be able to talk to distinguished epidemiologists, public health professionals and teachers. For more information, visit: *http://www.collegeboard.com/yes/.*

"The deadline for the final report for the YES competition is typically in February, so I would advise students interested in YES to begin seriously working on their project in September or October of the year prior. Students can enter as juniors or seniors and can enter more than once if they don't make it to the national level on their first try. To help come up with a research topic or idea, I would suggest browsing previous entries on the competition website *(www.collegeboard.com/yes).* Finally, to help streamline the process, I would advise students to focus on so-called hypothesis studies that ask a fairly narrow question: for example, does physical activity affect mood? Then, seek out the data you need to answer the question. In my experience, the most successful projects tend to keep that tight focus."
Aman Prasad: *First Place, Young Epidemiology Scholars Competition; Cornell Class of 2010*

I chose to pursue a YES project because it allowed me to pursue a passion, social analysis, through an interesting and relevant public health frame. I am not a future doctor, and will likely not be a professional within the public health field, but I had the freedom to make my YES project into something personally interesting, such that I was invested in it. I didn't have significant school or home resources beyond basic computing and a mathematical graphic application that I used to build the social network, but that was fine with the judges, because I still generated results.

My research could have failed to generate useful conclusions, and I still would have gained from the process. Make sure that your work is beneficial to you, even if you don't get any recognition, and you will be much happier in the long run. Neither you nor your parents are the best judges of how successful you will be. I remain amazed and grateful for my recognition, but in ten years, I'll treasure the memories of the YES weekend and of the actual research work more than the award. Don't set yourself up such that the research won't be worthwhile recognition.

Get help from a teacher or local professional, but don't be discouraged by a lack of support. As long as you have at least one person to keep you from wasting a week doing something unnecessary, you don't need much more. Embrace your creativity, and don't be afraid of failure. There's no better way to learn.
William L. Slack: *First Place, Young Epidemiology Scholars Competition; Williams Class of 2011*

"If you aspire to enter the field of public health, that is certainly a bonus. A large portion of the competition is focused around recruiting young minds to this important, but not necessarily popular, field. If that is not your calling, don't worry. It wasn't mine, and I did fine! Take the time to show why your research is important right now. Show the far-ranging impact of the problem you are addressing. Really know your stuff, as this was the competition at which I undoubtedly saw the highest quality of judging. These experts will drill you on anything, even if it is a small flaw in statistical analysis, so be able to back up everything you have done. If there is a unique part to your methodology, emphasize that. If you worked independently, emphasize that. The sensitive nature of my project didn't allow me to work in a lab, so even though I didn't have a lot of data, judges were very impressed that I put in all the extra time to recruit and test subjects and analyze data all by myself."
Ilana Rice: *Second Place, Young Epidemiology Scholars Competition; Finalist, Junior Science and Humanities Symposium; Semifinalist, Intel Science Talent Search; Barnard Class of 2013*

"The YES Competition is a three-day event that made an impact on my life, by reminding me of the importance of seeking advances in public health. To make the most of the YES experience, it's important to be very knowledgeable about your project and the specific details and definitions that factor into it. This can be especially difficult, given that the finalist round takes place in an auditorium in front of the other competitors and a panel of judges. Whereas local research competitions tend to have a one-on-one style, both for presentation and answering judges' questions, it's certainly more daunting to consider what a beta value represents when it is asked in front of peers, parents and advisors."

Chelsea Lynn Jurman: *Fifth Place, Intel Science Talent Search; Third Place, Young Epidemiology Scholars Competition; Yale Class of 2013*

sanofi-aventis International BioGENEius Challenge

Are you interested in developing assays to help detect and stop the spread of infectious diseases, engineering microbial fuel cells, or biotechnology in general? If you are, this competition is for you. The sanofi-aventis International BioGENEius Challenge is hosted by the Biotechnology Institute in collaboration with sanofi pasteur. Only projects in the field of biotechnology—defined as "the use of the knowledge of biological systems to produce goods and services"—qualify for this competition. A project can be deemed relevant if its content relates to various applications of biotechnology—such as health care, agriculture and forestry, food processing, mining and environment and forensics—and if it relies upon concepts in fields such as biochemistry, molecular biology, cell biology, microbiology and biotechnology. In order to participate, you must submit an application by mid-January. A judging committee will review the research project and select two individual finalists per state to advance to the United States' sanofi-aventis Regional BioGENEius Challenge. Students who are selected as regional finalists will each receive an all-expense paid trip to compete in the sanofi-aventis International BioGENEius Challenge in May/June. The competition coincides with the Biotechnology Industry Organization's (BIO) annual conference in cities such as Chicago (2010), Washington, D.C., (2011) and Boston (2012). The first place prize at the international level is $7,500; second place is $5,000; third place is $2,500; and fourth place is $1,000. This competition is similar in structure to the Siemens Competition, but is more focused on biotechnology. For more information visit: *http://www.biotechinstitute.org/programs/biogeneius_challenge.html.*

"This event is awesome to attend at the international level because it's not a traditional science fair; it's the world's largest biotechnology convention with a science fair attached. The exhibit floor is awe-inspiring, the speakers are famous and your awards ceremony is attended by thousands of people in charge of major biotech firms from across the world.

Judging in this event has a different feeling because it's done by industry professionals from some of the world's largest companies. They are smart people and most of them have done a lot of research in their past, so they grasp what you're doing pretty easily. Being businesspeople, though, they're also looking for projects with immediate applications to products, services or innovations in biotechnology.

The judges love to hear all the basic facts of your research to ensure that you've done your homework, but they also love to see how your research can be made into something with real-world applications. They usually ask some questions about the potential commercial application of your project—have you patented it? Have you considered who might be interested in buying a product from this research?

Public viewing day is also very cool at this event because the 'public' consists of thousands of researchers, companies and TV crews interested in biotechnology and your research. Take the opportunity to network with companies and other researchers who can help you expand your research and deliver it to the world."

Stephen Trusheim: *First Place, sanofi-aventis BioGENEius Challenge; Finalist, Intel Science Talent Search; First Place in Category, Intel International Science and Engineering Fair; Finalist, National Junior Science and Humanities Symposium; Regional Finalist, Young Epidemiology Scholars Competition; Semifinalist, Siemens Competition; Stanford Class of 2013*

"Three of the many criteria upon which projects are evaluated are "relevance to biotechnology," "validity of conclusions," and "level of science." In order to do well in this competition, from a presentation perspective, you should begin your presentation with a firm handshake, maintain a straight posture, make frequent eye contact with the judges, and use an appropriate volume for your voice relative to the distance from the judges. You should be aware that since the oral presentation is ten-minutes, only the most pertinent details pertaining to the objectives, results, conclusions and applications should be stressed as opposed to minor details pertaining to materials and methods or background information (although these should most definitely be mentioned). The oral presentation is one area where hand gestures are welcome and you shouldn't be afraid to let your passion and enthusiasm show. Applications to biotechnology and the relative significance of the project to mainstream society are major components of the evaluation, so you should identify and emphasize how your project relates to these areas. To make the most out of the BioGENEius experience you should socialize and interact with your fellow students as there is plenty of time between evaluations and outside of the actual competition where this is encouraged (ex. social events). Finally, the most important aspect of the entire BioGENEius competition is of course, to have fun!"

Ted Paranjothy: *First Place, sanofi-aventis BioGENEius Challenge; University of Manitoba Class of 2011*

"The competition is designed to give the younger generation a chance and opportunity in the industry, so capitalize on this and make the most of it. Be proud of what you do and present yourself well. Be confident and make sure you are well informed on the material you have covered. The opportunity to work and research in a scientific laboratory may never arise again, so be sure to learn as much as you can while you are there."

Oliver Tester: *Third Place, sanofi-aventis BioGENEius Challenge; University of Western Australia Class of 2012*

"The more well thought out your project, with an emphasis on the biotechnology applications, the more it will help you succeed in this competition. My experiences helped me understand how a professional career in research could be in my future. Currently I am participating in undergraduate research in biochemical engineering and hope to pursue an M.D./Ph.D. degree in the future."

Tejal U. Naik: *Third Place, sanofi-aventis BioGENEius Challenge; Third Place, Intel International Science and Engineering Fair; Semifinalist, Intel Science Talent Search; University of Delaware Class of 2011*

"This competition focuses on projects related to biotechnology/bioengineering. You'd be surprised how large of a field that is! Most projects are medicine related, but mine was environmental, and I'm sure you can come up another unique application!"
Rachel Ginn: *Fourth Place, sanofi-aventis BioGENEius Challenge; Arizona State University Class of 2012*

National Gallery for America's Young Inventors

Have you invented something that will change the world? If you have, the National Gallery for America's Young Inventors is for you. This venue is organized by the National Museum of Education (NMOE). It is the Hall of Fame that recognizes young American inventors whose "ideas have the potential to create a positive impact on our society." Each year the Gallery inducts six young people who created their invention or innovation while in grades K-12 and are no older than 19 at the time of induction. In order to be recognized, you need to fill out an application which will then be reviewed by a student board of advisers composed of pre-collegiate students. In order to qualify, one must be a U.S. citizen who has either been recognized in a national science competition, filed a patent (or has a patent pending) or has a product that is marketed nationally. The application is due on the date indicated on the website of the National Museum of Education. It varies each year based upon the date of induction. In addition to the honor and prestige of being inducted into the Gallery, you may win a U.S. Savings Bond, Edison Innovation Award and a display of your invention in Akron, Ohio. For more information, visit: *http://www.nmoe.org/gallery/index.htm/*.

"Beginning research at an earlier age starts the process of transferring critical-thinking skills to everything in life, and translates into adults who are better trained to look at their world and environment with more analytical eyes. The National Gallery for America's Young Inventors is meant to recognize, award and archive the achievements of students, in grades K-12, who have begun this process, and to provide a historic basis for future invention."
Leila Gay Evans: *Assistant Director, National Museum of Education*

"Once you have completed all of the hard work on a project, which meets the requirements for consideration by the National Gallery for America's Young Inventors, the most important part of competing for induction is your ability to communicate. There is no opportunity for the evaluators to ask questions, so it is important to thoroughly convey the project's usefulness, practicality, feasibility and marketability. It is important to include appropriate graphics and pictures that help to tell the story. Be concise. It is very difficult to keep an audience engaged while reading a technical paper. It is important to pull them in by expressing your excitement. Tell them why should they care or they will lose interest. In your application emphasize how your invention will benefit society. You have already proven the principles that make your project viable or you wouldn't be competing for induction. Now it is time to convince the audience that your product is worthy of their consideration."
Alexandra E. Crook: *Inductee, National Gallery for America's Young Inventors; Second Place in Engineering, Intel International Science and Engineering Fair; University of Utah Class of 2011*

"The National Gallery for America's Young Inventors looks for projects that have been recognized as solving real-world problems and for people who have a real passion for innovation and problem-solving.

The Gallery is all about practicality. The key questions that the judges ask about each project are, "Would this be useful?" and "Would I use or buy this?" The inventions that are chosen aren't always the most technologically advanced or the most complicated, because the judges aren't experts in your field of research; rather, they're also high school research-oriented students. Winning projects are most effective at tackling everyday problems and have a human-interest aspect that shows passion for practical problem-solving and inventing.

To do well in this competition, your application should explain in simple and clear terms what your invention does and why it's unique and award-worthy while also conveying your invention's basic technical aspects. Emphasize the practicality of your project and a human-interest component or something to differentiate it from the other projects submitted. Aside from a solid idea and paper, it also helps a lot if you've won previous awards in contests like ISEF, Siemens or STS or have a patent on your invention."

Michael Loy: *Inductee, National Gallery for America's Young Inventors; Finalist, Intel Science Talent Search; Second Place in Engineering, Intel International Science and Engineering Fair; Harvey Mudd College Class of 2013*

Additional Opportunities

Although we have highlighted a few of the well-known competitions, there are many more out there. Be on the look-out for local and state science competitions near your area. However, it cannot be overstated that winning competitions is not the ultimate purpose of your high school research experience; it is just an additional benefit!

"I believe if you do something well, the awards and recognition will follow on their own. There is really no secret to winning a competition, just follow your passion and research in topic matters that you are interested in. Follow the instructions for each competition and do a good job. If it involves a presentation, make sure you convey your message in an easy to follow manner that can be understood by the general public. If it involves essays, answer the questions they ask the best you can. At the very end it is not about the destination, but the amazing journey you travelled to get where you are today. Keep a high standard for your work, and recognition will follow."

Franz A. Sauer: *Third Place, National Junior Science and Humanities Symposium; Semifinalist, Siemens Competition; Caltech Class of 2012*

"It is often a matter of luck as to who finally wins these competitions. You can still be a very effective and productive scientist even if you do not win competitions. You should love doing the science regardless of winning a prize. Try again if you can."

Mary Ellen Stephen: *Veteran Research Teacher and President of the Massachusetts State Science Fair*

Take-Home Points

• Keep track of all the deadlines for these competitions in a planner. It can get hectic.
• Read the directions for each competition very carefully, because they're all different!.
• Search the web for more competitions.
• Each competition may look for something different in the winning projects.
• Visit the Archimedes Initiative *(www.archimedesinitiative.org)* to see the topical videos, "Judges" and "Best of Science Fair."

20

Summer Research Programs

Opportunity is missed by most people because it is dressed in overalls and looks like work.
Thomas A. Edison

Although summer may mean time to celebrate because school is out of session, it is also one of the best times to get involved in research. Conducting research during the school year is typically difficult because of time constraints and other limiting factors, such as transportation. Starting new research projects during the school year may be especially difficult because it takes a while to get used to the laboratory environment and develop relationships with your mentor and others in the lab (see Chapter 8: Working in a Laboratory).

The summer is an ideal time for motivated students to begin their research careers and for experienced students to dive into specific research projects. Participating in a research program is a great way to spend a summer and learn how to conduct independent research. It is important to start thinking about your summer plans in advance because many summer research programs have early application deadlines. Here are some of the popular research programs that helped many successful students begin or augment their research careers.

Research Science Institute (RSI)

> "RSI was incredible for meeting other young scientists. You may be the only one to do research at your high school, but it is great to know that there is a community of students like you across the country."
> **Maria Elena De Obaldia:** *Best of Category in Microbiology, Intel International Science and Engineering Fair; Regional Finalist, Siemens Competition; Research Science Institute Alumnus; Harvard Class of 2008*

The Research Science Institute (RSI) is an extraordinarily prestigious, intellectually rigorous, yet fun and memorable program that was founded by Admiral H.G. Rickover, father of the nuclear navy and Joann DiGennaro, President of the Center for Excellence in Education (CEE). Co-Sponsored by CEE and the Massachusetts Institute of Technology (MIT), RSI is a six-week, all-expenses-paid academic and research program. RSI enables 75 rising seniors to attend college-level classes and work with faculty members at MIT, Harvard and other institutions and corporations in the Boston area on research projects. Because of this, getting accepted into RSI is extremely competitive. The application requires essays, two recommendation letters, a high school transcript and applicable standardized testing scores (PSAT, SAT, ACT). It is suggested that PSAT math scores should be at least 75 and combined math, verbal, and writing scores should be at least 220. Selection into RSI is based on "intellectual merit and potential for leadership in science and technology." Applications are due in late January.

Once selected, RSI participants (so-called "Rickoids" after the founder of the Center for Excellence in Education, Admiral H.G. Rickover) attend on-campus cost-free classes in statistics, chemistry, biology and physics during the first week and then conduct research in designated laboratories throughout Boston for the following four weeks. During the last week of the program, each student develops an oral presentation and a written report. A panel of Boston-area scientists selects five papers and five presentations for special recognition at the end of the program. In addition to the research internships, there are distinguished speaker events that in the past have featured world-renowned scientists and mathematicians such as: Professor Noam Elkies, a three time Putnam Fellow in Mathematics; Professor Dudley Herschbach, Nobel laureate in chemistry; Professor Wolfgang Ketterle, Nobel laureate in physics; Professor Tom Leighton, co-founder of Akamai Technologies; ; David K. Rensin, founder of Reality Mobile, LLC; Professor Philip Sharp, Nobel laureate in physiology or medicine.

A summer at RSI is not all about science, however. One of the goals of RSI is to create a tight-knit community of young researchers that will continue throughout academic and professional careers. Additionally, many RSI participants enter science fairs, such as the Siemens Competition and Intel STS, and are very successful.

> "The program was amazing in terms of social aspects as well. The friends I made at RSI are unique, remarkable individuals from around the country and world. In between lectures and during our time outside the lab, I got to know my peers whether we were playing ping-pong or ultimate frisbee, or just watching Independence Day fireworks on the Charles River. Many of the relationships I formed with students and staff members at RSI have been invaluable to me and will likely last a lifetime."
> **Lauren R. Lisann:** *Finalist, Intel Science Talent Search; Semifinalist, Siemens Competition; Winner, American Academy of Neurology Neuroscience Research Prize; Research Science Institute Alumnus; Yale Class of 2012*

"I really loved RSI, especially because I met so many awesome people there. The research experience can be really amazing."
Mary Masterman: *First Place, Intel Science Talent Search; Best of Category in Physics, Intel International Science and Engineering Fair; Research Science Institute Alumnus; MIT Class of 2011*

"Although throughout high school I had been conducting my own independent research, I never really got to work in a science lab or experience the atmosphere of a research institution. RSI gave me the opportunity to see this facet of science research, one that will undoubtedly be increasingly prevalent depending on what type of career I pursue. Of course, first and foremost, it was a learning experience in the scientific sense, and I got a first-class exposure to the field of human genetics. But more than that, I got a glimpse of what goes on in the "real world" of science labs through my internship.

Outside of the internship, the RSI program brought together a group of the brightest and most ambitious students in the fields of math, science and engineering. I had a great time getting to know the other students and made many friends that I'll likely keep in contact with through college. The RSI program also taught us how to use various applications for the purpose of presentation and brought various speakers to explain their careers and achievements. Overall, the whole experience really reconstructed what I considered to be 'science'."
Nolan Kamitaki: *Davidson Fellow; Second Place in Medicine and Health, Intel International Science and Engineering Fair; Semifinalist, Intel Science Talent Search; Semifinalist, Young Epidemiology Scholars Competition; Finalist, Junior Science and Humanities Symposium; Waiakea High School Class of 2010*

For more information visit *http://www.cee.org/rsi/download.shtml.*

Program in Mathematics for Young Scientists (PROMYS)

Do problems in mathematics excite you more than, say, cloning DNA? If so then the Program in Mathematics for Young Scientists (PROMYS) might be the right program for you. This six-week program at Boston University is designed for students to explore and answer challenging questions in mathematics. Students are advised by some of the most talented undergraduate math majors in the country who are attending top colleges such as Harvard, MIT, Caltech and Princeton. Beginning participants attend lectures on number theory in the morning and solve problem sets in smaller groups throughout the remainder of the day. They devise their own mathematical proofs under the guidance of counselors. First year students can also meet in groups working on exploration research projects. More experienced participants join advanced seminars in abstract algebra, geometry and symmetry, and modular forms; or they may work on research projects with visiting faculty mentors. Because some of the brightest minds in the country are at this program, PROMYS is not like your ordinary high school math class. This is where math moves towards research. It should be noted that PROMYS and RSI share a rivalry that culminates in an annual Ultimate Frisbee game.

For more information, visit *http://www.promys.org/*.

CURE Internship at Dana-Farber/Harvard Cancer Center

> "The experience was truly invaluable. I enjoyed working with my mentor so much that I continued working there throughout the school year. I am very grateful for the bridge that the internship helped to build between us and the leading scientists in the world."
>
> **Xiaoli Mi:** *Finalist, Intel International Science and Engineering Fair; Harvard Class of 2012*

> "My participation in the CURE program has made an impact on both my academic and extracurricular pursuits. I am putting to use many of the techniques my research lab taught me."
>
> **Blessing Agunwamba:** *Princeton Class of 2010*

The Continuing Umbrella of Research Experiences (CURE) program introduces high school and college students from underrepresented populations to the world of cancer research by placing them in real research settings at local cancer research institutions. Its goal is to encourage students to pursue future careers in the biosciences—particularly cancer research—giving practical meaning to academic course work. At the same time, students make a valuable contribution to the Dana Farber/Harvard Cancer Center (DF/HCC) research mission. By participating in a program at DF/HCC—an NCI comprehensive cancer center with more than 1,000 researchers across seven major Harvard institutions—students will learn from experts who are devoted to preventing, treating and curing cancer. Each year, a number of promising students are selected for this unique opportunity to expand and extend their interest in basic, clinical or population science cancer research or nursing.

During the nine-week summer program, students will participate in a seminar series on scientific research and professional development to familiarize students with relevant medical initiatives, new training technology, treatment and psychosocial issues of cancer patients, potential career paths and other topics. In addition, students will learn how to read scientific papers and be exposed to biomedical research tools. Writing, speaking and presentation skills are developed. A series of networking and social activities facilitates participants meeting other students who are also interested in biomedical research.

For more information, visit *http://www.dfhcc.harvard.edu/center-initiatives/iecd/ student-training/cure-program/* or contact Elizabeth Zdunich at *elizabeth_zdunich@ dfci.harvard.edu*.

Research Scholar Program at Garcia MRSEC

This program is ideal for students interested in material science and nanotechnology. Garcia's Research Scholar Program provides the opportunity for students to participate in polymer and bioengineering research. The students are taught research skills that are valuable in the field and many continue to enter science fairs. The program begins on June 30 and continues until August 15. Students will be able to conduct research at SUNY Stony Brook, Polytechnic University, CUNY and North Carolina State University. The application process requires your academic information, transcript, three letters of recommendation and essay answers. The program consists of a lecture series in materials science and nanotechnology and a poster presentation day.

For more information, visit *http://polymer.matscieng.sunysb.edu/researchscholar. htm.*

Rockefeller University's Summer Outreach Program

"I participated in Rockefeller University's Summer Outreach Program for high school students as a 16 year-old. My research project itself wasn't particularly productive, but I got to work with a fantastic mentor. I had a lot of fun and a fairly free reign, pursuing my fairly unlikely goal using any methods I could come up with. The program included a weekly session with other high school students; it was a great opportunity to share stories, concerns and lab progress. I learned how to dissect a published research paper and how to put together a PowerPoint, a research paper and a very basic poster—and I made friends that I still keep in touch with!"
Alicia Darnell: *Second Place, Siemens Competition; Best of Category in Medicine and Health, Intel International Science and Engineering Fair; National Finalist, Junior Science and Humanities Symposium; Yale Class of 2012*

The Rockefeller University's Summer High School Science Outreach Program (SOP) is a program for "engaged, intellectually curious and highly motivated high school students with a strong aptitude in the life or physical sciences" to experience laboratory research. Each year, 40 high school students are chosen to participate in the program and are matched to labs according to their field of interest. During the seven-week program, students will participate in a summer research project. In order to apply, you must be at least 16 years old at the start of the program.

For more information, visit *http://www.rockefeller.edu/outreach/highschoolapp.php.*

Summer Science Program (SSP)

"Two years ago I attended Summer Science Program (SSP), a six-week long astronomy camp. It's one of those work hard, play hard type experiences. You learn calculus, a lot of physics, how to program in Python, how to observe asteroids with a telescope and how to survive without sleep for extended periods of time. It was amazing. SSP was an experience that gave me a taste of what college might be like and it solidified my interest in science research. I would highly recommend it! You can apply after your junior year of high school with a couple short essays and a reference."
Erika Alden DeBenedictis: *Davidson Fellow; First Place, Intel Science Talent Search; Best of Category in Team, Intel International Science and Engineering Fair; Third Place Team, Siemens Competition; Caltech Class of 2014*

The Summer Science Program is a six-week program for gifted high school juniors that features a hands-on research project in celestial mechanics. This program focuses on astronomy, physics, calculus and programming. Students take classes in these subjects and learn to collect and analyze data from telescopic observations of asteroids. SSP takes place at New Mexico Tech in Socorro (June 15-July 26) and Besant Hill School in Ojai, California (June 22-August 2). Only high school juniors taking or planning on taking calculus are invited to apply, although a handful of advanced sophomores are occasionally selected into the program for a total of 36 students. SSP is looking for gifted high school students with standardized test scores that place them in the top ten percent in math and the top 25 percent in verbal/reading. They are also looking for scientific pursuits outside of the classroom. According to their website, SSP "takes into account any personal or family circumstances that may have presented obstacles to your academic achievements. The application will provide an opportunity for you to explain your unique background and situation." Applications will need to include your grades, standardized test scores, essay answers, official transcript and two teacher recommendations. One downside is that the program fee is $3,850 for the summer, although generous financial aid is available. The Summer Science Program is a great program for students interested in physics and astronomy to gain field experience and explore the universe.

For more information, visit *http://www.summerscience.org.*

Stanford Institutes of Medicine Summer Research Program (SIMR)

If you are interested in hands-on research in various fields of medicine (immunology, cancer, stem cell, neuroscience and cardiovascular medicine), you should definitely apply to the Stanford Institutes of Medicine Summer Research Program. Started in 2000, SIMR selects about 40 high school students (current juniors and seniors) from schools primarily in California (but out-of-state students are welcome to apply) to conduct research with leading scientists. Housing is not offered through the program. In addition to conducting research, the students attend informative lectures given by Stanford faculty and graduate students. The culmination of this exciting eight-week research program is the student poster presentation on campus.

For more information, visit *http://simr.stanford.edu/.*

Young Engineering and Science Scholars (YESS)

YESS! The Young Engineering and Science Scholars (YESS) research program is a three-week residential summer program at Caltech for exceptional underrepresented high school students. The goal of this program is to expose students to the "excitement and rigor of science research" and to create a community of student researchers. As part of the program, the participants will go to lectures, conduct hands-on experiments, complete project work, attend a computer programming workshop and listen to research presentations and lab tours all led by Caltech graduate students. In addition, the students will complete group research projects mentored by graduate students and postdoctoral scholars. YESS also includes a faculty lecture series with several Nobel Prize winners, and tours of Caltech's state-of-the-art research facilities including the NASA Jet Propulsion Laboratory (JPL). Aside from research, students will be able to attend college admissions workshops with tips directly from the Caltech admissions officers. This program is not all about research, though. YESS will take you on field trips around Southern California. What more could you want out of three weeks of research and fun?

For more information, visit *http://www.yess.caltech.edu/index.html*.

Spending the Summer on Your Own

Do not be disappointed if you are not able to participate in a formally organized summer research program. There are many ways to get involved in summer research and still have a memorable time. One way is to get involved in a laboratory near your home (see Chapter 7: Finding a Lab and a Mentor. Researching during the summer, independently of a program, is often more flexible and affords you more time to actually do your research. Since you will not have classes to worry about, this is the ideal time to develop a strong relationship with your mentor. Try to develop a long-term research project that you may want to continue during the year. You should focus on learning as much as you can about your field of interest and also learning what other people are working on in the lab. Understanding the focus and vision of the lab is important and may help you figure out exactly where your interests lie. But do not spend all your time working in the lab. It is the summer after all!

> "I did not specifically participate in research programs over the summer, but I definitely used the summer as an opportunity to work on my research. I interned at a local veteran's organization, which gave me time and resources to recruit several participants. The initiative to get out in the community and do work on my research even though it was not through a program was definitely something that impressed judges at competitions. So even if you don't get into a program, don't let that stop you!"
>
> **Ilana Rice:** *Second Place, Young Epidemiology Scholars Competition; Finalist, Junior Science and Humanities Symposium; Semifinalist, Intel Science Talent Search; Barnard Class of 2013*

Take-Home Points

- There are many programs for you to choose from to keep yourself busy over the summer.
- Start your applications to summer programs well in advance.
- Look for research opportunities near your area if you would like to do research independent of a program.
- Have fun! It's the summer!

Part V:
Research Beyond High School

21

Research After High School

Don't ask yourself what the world needs. Ask yourself what makes you come alive and then go do that. Because what the world needs is people who have come alive.
Howard Thurman

After you have conducted your first research project, you should have a better idea whether continuing to do research in college is something that interests you. College research likely will be similar to high school research; however, there are some unique aspects of college research worth noting. Depending on what you are planning to do after college, you may decide that it is worth your while to devote a significant amount of time to research. Alternatively, you may decide to focus on your coursework and several extracurricular activities. This is not to say that you cannot do all these things; however, conducting research will take some of your time away from your studies. Kelley Harris, who attended Harvard College, said, "research competes for my time with so many equally appealing things in college, which were just not available to me in high school. I love research, but I also like to spend a lot of time on classes, and I now have trouble dividing my attention between research and classes if I work during the school year."

You will want to plan ahead and choose your courses to accommodate your research. Consider the difficulty and time commitments required for your course load and try to anticipate whether you will be able to devote time to research on top of your courses. If you are taking two difficult science requirements with many hours of required laboratory time during the fall semester, it may be best to wait until the spring semester to start working on a research project. Find out whether independent or supervised research is required for your major and then ask around about how and during what semester students typically fulfill this requirement. Summer may be an ideal time to pursue research in college, especially if your college has a residential program or available funding. Many students will choose to do research for credit during their junior years or during the summer before senior year, in order to get a head start on their senior thesis research projects. Usually you will have the option of doing research for course credit or for pay, if funds are available. All the advantages of conducting research, such as contact with faculty and the valuable research it provides, make doing research as a job an attractive option, as opposed to a job that would not necessarily expand your horizons.

If you have already done research in high school, you will likely be able to transition smoothly into research in the college environment. In fact, many of the barriers you may have faced in high school will disappear. For example, you should have access to many professors on your campus who routinely take on undergraduate students as research assistants. Possible mentors are all around you: your advisors, professors from your courses and their colleagues. Ask your advisor about which professors in your field have reputations for mentoring undergraduates, since this will not be the case for all professors. Approach a would-be mentor with the same courtesy and savvy you used to secure a mentor in high school (see Chapter 7).

If your college has an undergraduate research club, join it to meet other people with similar interests. Find out if your major has a central office or advisor for students interested in conducting supervised or independent research. This advisor will be able to tell you about funding opportunities. Many colleges will have numerous grants available for research, especially for students who plan to write senior theses. Find out about deadlines far in advance, so that you have time to approach a mentor if you do not already have one, and to devise a suitable project. In order to get funding, you have to have a well-thought out idea to write about in your proposal, and usually you need to show that you have a professor willing to supervise your work. Organizations outside your school are also good sources of funding and may sponsor summer programs for undergraduates. For students in the biological sciences, the Howard Hughes Medical Institute (HHMI) and the National Institutes of Health (NIH) sponsor and fund summer programs. The National Science Foundation (NSF) sponsors the Research Experiences for Undergraduates (REU) program for U.S. citizens and permanent residents. Students may apply to an REU Site to do research in a variety of different disciplines. If accepted, students will receive a stipend and are paired with a suitable advisor with similar interests.

Competitions analogous to those that exist for high school researchers are much less common in the college years; however, there are opportunities for you to share your research with others and in many cases, to earn recognition. For example, Microsoft Research sponsors the Association for Computing Machinery (ACM) Student Research competition for undergraduate and graduate students. Find out whether a research symposium exists at your school, where students can display posters of their research; if not, consider starting one (see Chapter 23). Your school may also have a science journal of its own or a science review, where you can share your own research or write about the research of others that interests you. There are many ways to get involved in your college's research community if you look for them. You will also likely have many opportunities to attend seminars and scientific talks by professors at your school and visiting professors. Take advantage of these opportunities to broaden your horizons and meet new people.

In college you may decide to continue in the same field as you did your high school research, but you may consider exploring other fields. After college and beyond, there will be plenty of time to build up expertise in your chosen field. At this early stage in your career it is a good idea not to narrow your focus too much, since a broad education can be useful in determining your true research interests and informing later research in your chosen field of study. Kelley Harris conducted high school research in biology, which led to a third place win at the Intel Science Talent Search. Upon entering Harvard as a freshman later that year, with high school research experience under her belt, she treated her undergraduate years *as a fun exploration opportunity.* Kelley majored in mathematics, because she found its methods *"addicting."* Meanwhile, she worked in biology research groups and took many courses in English and history. Kelley's experience solidified her reasons for wanting to apply to graduate school: "I have much better reasons for choosing [my field] than I did when I was 15, and I have many new intellectual perspectives to offer the field. I know what it's like to focus and I know what it's like to drift among many intellectual passions, and I wouldn't feel comfortable applying to graduate school without having first experienced both modes of being."

If you enjoy doing research in high school and college, you should look into the possibility of pursuing a graduate level education, such as a master's degree or doctoral degree, such as a Ph.D., in your chosen area of study. In the United States, most science Ph.D. programs are federally funded and thus, cover tuition and research expenses, in addition to providing a stipend to cover the student's living expenses. If getting paid to go to school and do research sounds like a dream come true, graduate school may be the right path for you. Graduate school can be very demanding and requires a great deal of personal time commitment; however, it can be especially rewarding because your experience can be tailored to your unique interests and learning needs. Talk to your college's teaching assistants and professors to learn more about what graduate school is like and how to prepare for the graduate school application process. Unlike professional schools such as medical school or law school, the time it takes to graduate from a Ph.D. program is not pre-determined and depends on many factors, including the time it takes to finish coursework and a research-based independent thesis project. A panel of professors, called a thesis committee, oversees student research. The student's work is also closely monitored by the thesis advisor or mentor. The student's advisor and thesis committee determine when the student has demonstrated the intellectual growth and accomplished enough to write and orally defend the thesis, and ultimately, to graduate. Completion of a Ph.D. can take anywhere from three to six years or even longer. Graduate education generally prepares students for careers in academia, such as becoming a college or university professor, but it can also open doors in many "non-academic" or industry jobs.

Take-Home Points

- Research entails different expectations, challenges and benefits at different levels: high school, college and medical/graduate school.
- Generally, as you progress, the level of time and intellectual investment that is expected increases. Additionally, as you gain experience, more independence is granted, allowing you to explore personal interests. This freedom is the most rewarding and challenging aspect of advanced research.
- Be open to new experiences and honest with yourself about what makes you happy and excites you. Bring rigor and enthusiasm to everything you do to increase your chances for success.

22

Conferences and Papers

A scientist shouldn't be asked to judge the economic and moral value of his work.
All we should ask the scientist to do is find the truth—and then not keep it from anyone.
Arthur Kornberg

A major indicator of success in the scientific and broader academic community is the frequency with which one publishes his or her work and how often one is invited to present at conferences. Written and oral communication continue to be critical to successful research at the highest levels of academia, just as they are important to your success in high school research and competitions. Sharing your findings with others in your field can be very rewarding, and indeed this form of cooperation is important for fueling new discoveries and progress in science. Integrity is highly valued in science; it is imperative that scientists represent their work as accurately as possible and acknowledge the limitations of their work, especially in publications and presentations.

If you have discovered something novel during your research, you may be able to prepare a manuscript of your work for submission to a peer-reviewed journal. Your mentor or professor will be able to tell you whether your work is suitable for publication, and if so, they can advise you when and how to submit your work. After you submit your manuscript, it will be reviewed by experts in your particular field, who will either recommend or not recommend it for publication. Next, the reviewers will provide the authors with comments on the strengths and weaknesses of the manuscript. The authors then have an opportunity to address reviewer comments and questions. Sometimes reviewers stipulate that additional experiments need to be conducted before a manuscript can be accepted for publication. The time between submission and publication can vary from several months to a year. If you plan to submit your work for publication, it is even more important that you keep careful records and keep your data in order throughout the course of your experiment, so that you are able to prepare an accurate and high-quality manuscript describing the work. You should identify target journals for your manuscript with your mentor's guidance, and read previously published articles in these journals to get a feeling for the content, style, length and format of articles in that particular journal. All journals are not created equal. You should conduct a thorough literature search in your field, so that you are aware of what, if anything, has been published recently about your topic. From time to time, certain research problems in every field become "hot," and if you happen to be working on one of these particular questions at the right time, you will likely have an easier time getting your work published. Similarly, the reputation of your mentor as a leader in his or her field will lend credibility to your work and make it more likely to be published.

When you have made a novel finding, you should make it public to others working in your field. Publications are the currency of science, they help you to progress in your career and to engage with your field. Just as your work builds upon previous work done by others, your findings may inspire someone else's research.

Research is a competitive business, since funding resources are limited. At times researchers may be selective about sharing their work before it is published, lest someone "steal" their idea. Keep this in mind when sharing, since any work done under the supervision of your mentor belongs to him or her, to some extent. While this is the reality of academic science in the 21st century, it is good scientific practice to be transparent, honest and rigorous in the publication of your findings. Concealing or misrepresenting information does not show integrity. At times, published data needs to be retracted because it is proven to be wrong or cannot be replicated by others; however, this is rare. The integrity and quality of the scientific literature depends on the integrity of scientists. In other words, it is important that you are thoroughly convinced of anything that you plan to publish. Be your own devil's advocate: think of experiments that would prove your conclusions wrong and do those experiments. If you are right, this information will only make your data more convincing. If your research is in a popular field, others are sure to repeat your experiments and challenge your hypothesis at some point in the future. Thus, it is best for you to understand any weaknesses in your data before publication, rather than afterwards. Your research mentors gained their positions and reputations by consistently producing research that is of high quality and which their peers can trust as accurate. It is important that you uphold this tradition. As a researcher, you may face pressure to generate exciting data that fits your hypothesis (or your mentors'); however, always remember that the most important mission of a scientist is to uncover the truth and let this guide you through every step of every experiment and your data analysis.

Academic and professional conferences generally occur once a year and are held in a different city each year. Professors in a particular field will organize the professional conference and most look forward to this opportunity to share their work with others and learn about what their colleagues are studying. This is a fantastic opportunity to get to know the key players in your field of research and to engage with the scientific community.

Science becomes more fun once you can match faces to the names you read in books and publications. Organizers are under pressure to hold a conference that attendees think is interesting and informative. Thus, organizers are always looking for professors, and sometimes postdoctoral fellows, graduate students or undergraduates who are excellent presenters, so that they can invite them to speak at their conferences. High school students rarely are asked to present at a conference; however, if this is something you are interested in doing, you should consult your mentor about what opportunities are available. Often times conference organizers will ask that you submit a concise abstract about your research and they will use these to select speakers and poster presentations. Being chosen to present your work at a conference is an honor and indicates that others are interested in your work. For example, after submitting an abstract, Kelley Harris was invited to present her work at the Joint Mathematics Meeting as an undergraduate at Harvard. It is a rare honor to be invited to speak as an undergraduate, and even as a graduate student, at some conferences. Take every opportunity you get to present your work to different audiences, whether at conferences, seminars, in classes or lab meeting. The ability to present yourself and your work in a positive light is invaluable, no matter what field you choose to enter.

Take-Home Points

- Publications and invitations to give talks about your research are the currency of science and a critical way to gain recognition and funding for your research.
- Hold yourself to the highest standards of integrity in conducting and publishing accurate, technically sound research. When in doubt, assume that you are wrong and figure out how to convince yourself of your data.
- Take every opportunity you are given to present your work, and always prepare yourself to inform and engage your audience. Being able to communicate about science in oral and written form has invaluable benefits to you and your career.

23

Finding a Research Community on Campus

We must remember that one determined person can make a significant difference, and that a small group of determined people can change the course of history.
Sonia Johnson

If you are interested in science and research, it is important to find a research community on campus. Oftentimes students in college start doing research only as juniors or seniors because they are not encouraged earlier. A research community, like Harvard College's Undergraduate Research Association (HCU-RA), can bring in faculty to talk to students about research opportunities and also help you network with your peers. Research organizations also hold symposia and other events that showcase undergraduate research projects. If there is no such community on your campus, it may be worthwhile to find other students who share your interest in research and starting one at your college.

The Importance of Community

Scientists have the unfortunate stereotype of being introverts whose interactions with living beings are limited to the lab rats they work with. This is a flawed impression (for the most part) because it has become increasingly important for researchers to interact with one another. Research is becoming more interdisciplinary, and progress is often the result of collaborations among scientists in different fields. Professional researchers form communities of anywhere between five to hundreds of thousands of members so they can keep abreast of the latest research developments in their field and form collaborations. These large professional organizations include the American Association for the Advancement of Science, Sigma Xi , and field-specific organizations, like the Society for Neuroscience; each organization holds an annual conference and publishes a journal (AAAS—*Science*, Sigma Xi—*American Scientist*, SfN—*Journal of Neuroscience*). These professional associations also have student membership options which can be quite helpful. It can be very beneficial for you to become part of a research community as an undergraduate in order to develop as a scientist and form professional contacts that may be helpful in the future.

Undergraduate Research Associations

> "The Harvard College Undergraduate Research Association has been doing an excellent job in promoting scientific research on campus. They have been organizing great talks by prominent figures in science, and the annual [Harvard Undergraduate Research Symposium] has been working very well for the undergraduate body."
> **Leslie Beh:** *Best of Category in Microbiology, Intel International Science and Engineering Fair; Research Science Institute; Harvard Class of 2011*

Most colleges unfortunately do not have research associations, so undergraduate researchers may go through their whole college career without interacting with any of their peers. You may be wondering, 'Is this really a bad thing?' The answer is a resounding yes, even if you decide later that a research career is not for you. An undergraduate research association is far more than an extracurricular venue to meet your peers. These groups have broad purposes that include: 1) connecting students with research opportunities; 2) showcasing undergraduate research via symposia and publications; and 3) hosting faculty or other distinguished guests for research lectures. The main activities of undergraduate research associations are highlighted below.

Research Opportunities

One of the main functions of a research association is to provide information about term-time and summer research opportunities. These include open research positions and summer research programs for undergraduates, which number in the hundreds if not thousands (e.g., the National Science Foundation's Research Experience for Undergraduate programs). Some research associations even have advising programs where experienced upperclassmen researchers are paired with freshmen or sophomores who have no idea how to get started. These mentors help their peers find labs, write emails to potential mentors and apply for research grants, among many other things. All of the authors of this guide have been mentors for HCURA's Research Advising Program. Another opportunity that research associations provide is developmental workshops that cover topics such as writing cogent research grants, giving presentations to technical or public audiences and publishing research papers.

Symposia

There are no large science competitions like ISEF for undergraduates. This is good because as you progress in your career you will find that science is not a competition to be judged by a third party; rather, it is a collaboration, and the sole judge of its merit is whether it stands the test of time and becomes fact or law. Of course there are competitive aspects to professional research, such as filing patents and publishing research findings first, but they are not as directly competitive as science fairs. Fairs and competitions are replaced by symposia and conferences. Many colleges now have research symposia which aim to showcase student research. Organizing symposia is one of the main priorities of undergraduate research associations because these events are the main venue to show professors, peers and the public what undergraduate researchers have accomplished. These symposia are also breeding grounds for collaborative ideas and, as such, usually feature poster sessions, plenary speakers and abstract books.

Publications

If you take a trip to any scientific library at a college, you will immediately be amazed at the endless number of journals on subjects ranging from plate tectonics to virology. There are easily thousands of scientific publications; some of them are obscure and are read by an audience of fewer than the number of staff needed to publish the journal, others are quite well-known and influential, like Science and Nature. While it is definitely possible for enterprising high school and college students to publish their work in professional journals, it is not as common as we would like, due to the intense peer review process (e.g., Science accepts less than ten percent of the research manuscripts that it receives).

Fortunately there are a number of undergraduate journals that focus on student research and will accept your work contingent upon their own peer review. Undergraduate research associations often publish their own journals or publicize other journals to their members. There are a growing number of undergraduate publications; for example, MIT, Harvard, Stanford and Rice—to name a few—all have thriving undergraduate research journals. Generally, these are also high-quality publications because they are edited by undergraduates who are advised by professors or even an entire faculty board. If your college does not have an undergraduate research journal, you can start your own or contribute to larger journals. An online, international journal known as the Journal of Young Investigators (www.jyi.org) is a popular venue to publish undergraduate research and to meet other undergraduate researchers across the world.

Guest Lectures

The most inspiring talks during your college years are often outside of the classroom. These are given by guest lectures, usually faculty members, who normally discuss exciting developments in a field as well as their own research. It is much more stimulating to learn about the recent procedure for slowing down the speed of light (as was the topic of one Harvard College

Undergraduate Research Association (HCURA) guest lecture) than it is to work through Maxwell's Equations with a paper and pencil, though the latter is crucial to your fundamental knowledge as a scientist and the former is important to maintain your enthusiasm for research. However, these guest lectures normally are organized by the departments within the college and there are no opportunities for students themselves to bring in faculty they want to hear. Undergraduate research associations may serve as a bridge between students and faculty because they have the formal status needed to host an event. Faculty lectures are not only great ways to learn about developments in various fields, they allow you to meet distinguished faculty in small groups and perhaps even discuss ideas or express your desire to join their labs.

No Research Community on Campus? Start Your Own!

If your college does not have an undergraduate research association, it is entirely possible to start one! There are a few initial steps that you must take. First, you must research what it takes to start a student organization on campus. Do you need faculty advisors, a minimum number of initial members, a projected budget, et cetera? Next, you must generate interest among fellow undergraduate researchers and start building a board for the association. Having a faculty advisor or two can be really helpful in focusing the goals of the organization and recruiting more members to the association. For example HCURA has the support of Dudley Herschbach, who won the Nobel Prize in chemistry; this helped to excite other students to attend HCURA events. Once approved, your college's research association should begin holding at least monthly events—guest lectures, developmental workshops, symposia, and so on. The more opportunities the research association provides, the more members it will have to start new and exciting initiatives. In the future, your college's research association can, and should, collaborate with those of other colleges on things such as community-wide symposia and research exchanges. Your involvement with a research association can be one of the most, if not the most, meaningful experience of your college career.

Take-Home Points

- Research is becoming increasingly interdisciplinary. Major scientific advances are often the product of collaborations.
- It is important to be part of a research community, such as an undergraduate research association.
- Undergraduate research associations can connect you with research opportunities, help you showcase your research via symposia and publications and organize talks by faculty or other distinguished guests.

24

Afterword

Dr. Lisa Randall
Frank B. Baird, Jr. Professor of Science, Harvard University; First Tenured Female Professor in the Princeton University Physics Department and First Tenured Female Theoretical Physicist at MIT and Harvard; First Place, 1980 Westinghouse Science Talent Search

Research is an experience like no other. Most people will never have the chance to engage in this activity. Even those students who ultimately decide to study science will probably have to wait several years before experiencing the joys and frustration of this endeavor.

The students who wrote this book had the pleasure and rewards of doing research projects in high school. They participated in science competitions that changed their lives. Most fields of science require years of preparation before one is able to advance the forefront of knowledge, yet they found ways as high school students to learn enough to participate. And they decided to share some of what they learned along the way with you.

Choosing a project and successfully executing it to completion are very different challenges, and the authors of this book have tried to give their perspectives on both. It is critical to find a topic that truly absorbs you sufficiently that you'll want to learn about the state of the field and devote your time and energy to a project that can help move it forward. The project you choose should allow you to experience some of the joys of having an idea, seeing it through, and discovering something for yourself. If you devote time and energy to this activity, it should be some idea or activity that stimulates your mind and challenges you with new ideas and skills.

Research is what you will ultimately do as a scientist, and it involves skills that overlap with, but differ from, those that you use in a classroom. When you take your classes, it will be extraordinarily valuable to have the perspective that a good research experience can bring. Learning is always fun, but trying to answer a question that no one has answered before probably comes closer to the reason you decided to do science in the first place. It is amazing to know what you are looking forward to and where it is heading. It is also valuable to have the confidence that a successful research project can bring. Sharing first place for my number theory project in what was then the Westinghouse Science Competition was an experience that, even when I had doubts, I could count on to propel me forward.

Keep in mind that although the authors of this book did their best to share their experience and advice, each research activity is unique. The contents are not rules and you should not think something is wrong because your research does not precisely conform to a set pattern. These students are providing guidelines and advice that they hope you can use to facilitate and enrich your experience. You can best respond to their guidance, however, by thinking for yourself and choosing what is most helpful.

Any creative endeavor can teach you a great deal. The perspective you get from creating something new enhances anything else you learn about a research or creative area. I had many opportunities in the world of particle physics. One thing I particularly like about my research is that I have the opportunity to work on many different projects ranging from the interior of matter to the expanses of the cosmos. I can think about details of the so-called Standard Model of particle physics, that tells us about matter's most basic elements and interactions, and propose interesting ways to learn more about its properties. I can also consider exotic new ideas—or models as we call them—that experimenters can go look for, such as ideas about an extra dimension of space. And I can interact with experimenters to suggest new signatures to look for, or new ways to look for old ones. Plus I get to extend my interests to cosmology, including dark matter and how an excess of matter over antimatter was created. As a professor, the opportunity to share research ideas with new students makes the research experience even more worthwhile.

Your scientific goals are probably paramount, but learning to present your work to others will prove to be an important skill as well—one that will help you no matter what you ultimately choose to pursue. The opportunity to engage the public through writing and speaking about my book, *Warped Passages: Unraveling the Mysteries of the Universe's Hidden Dimensions*, and a book currently in progress, entitled *Knocking on Heaven's Door*, has been both useful and enjoyable. Writing gave me firsthand experience explaining challenging but technically useful ideas. Public engagement also brought me into contact with artists and composers who provided different and valuable perspectives on and enriched my thinking about culture and the relationship between science and the arts. I even had the opportunity to write a libretto for a small "projective opera."

Sharing your results and ideas—along with your research itself—will teach you lessons about doing creative things on your own, provide an important opportunity to reflect more deeply about your research and its implications, and give you the skills to interact and collaborate with people outside your field. All of these experiences will be useful no matter what you end up doing in life.

Happily, all these activities give the pleasure of creating something new. So get started, enjoy your research, and have fun. You are about to enter a great adventure.

Appendix: Useful Web Resources

Resources

The Archimedes Initiative

www.archimedesinitiative.org

The Archimedes Initiative is focused on strengthening science literacy and increasing the number of scientists and engineers in the United States. They have chosen competitive science fairs as the starting place for demonstrating and describing the joy and energy that surrounds self discovery and experimentation. Science Fairs, experimentation, engineering projects, health studies, computer programming and psychological studies all provide a means for students and others to direct their own interests while learning and experiencing at their own pace. The Archimedes Initiative features excellent video interviews of high school researchers on a range of topics related to the chapters in this guide.

Research Corporation for Science Advancement (RCSA)

www.rescorp.org

Research Corporation for Science Advancement is an active, hands-on foundation that stimulates advances in science. Its role is catalytic rather than controlling. Its mission is one of partnership rather than ownership. Among its many activities, RCSA publishes books related to promoting science advancement in society.

Society for Science & the Public (SSP)

www.societyforscience.org

Society for Science & the Public (SSP) is dedicated to public engagement in scientific research and education. Its vision is to promote the understanding and appreciation of science and the vital role it plays in human advancement: to inform, educate, inspire. SSP is responsible for the ISEF and STS competitions, among others, as well as publishing *Science News*.

Science Buddies

www.sciencebuddies.org

Science Buddies offers free science fair project ideas, answers and tools for serious students. It is a great resource for anyone looking to take full advantage of the science opportunities available.

Competitions

Intel International Science and Engineering Fair (ISEF)

www.societyforscience.org/isef/

Siemens Competition

www.siemens-foundation.org/en/competition.htm
www.collegeboard.com/siemens/index.html

Intel Science Talent Search (STS)
www.societyforscience.org/sts

Davidson Fellows
www.davidsongifted.org/fellows

Junior Science and Humanities Symposium (JSHS)
www.jshs.org

American Junior Academy of Science (AJAS)
www.amjas.org.

Young Epidemiology Scholars (YES) Competition
www.collegeboard.com/yes/.

Sanofi-aventis International BioGENEius Challenge
www.biotechinstitute.org/programs/biogeneius_challenge.html

National Gallery for America's Young Inventors
www.nmoe.org/gallery/index.htm

Summer Programs

Research Science Institute (RSI)
www.cee.org/rsi/download.shtml

Program in Mathematics for Young Scientists (PROMYS)
www.promys.org

CURE Internship at Dana-Farber/Harvard Cancer Center
www.dfhcc.harvard.edu/center-initiatives/iecd/student-training/cure-program

Research Scholar Program at Garcia MRSEC
polymer.matscieng.sunysb.edu/researchscholar.htm

Rockefeller University's Summer Outreach Program
www.rockefeller.edu/outreach/highschoolapp.php

Summer Science Program (SSP)
www.summerscience.org

Stanford Institutes of Medicine Summer Research Program (SIMR)
simr.stanford.edu

Young Engineering and Science Scholars (YESS)
www.yess.caltech.edu/index.html

About the Authors

Shiv Gaglani

Shiv Gaglani is a member of the Harvard Class of 2010. As an undergraduate he studied biomedical sciences and engineering as well as health policy, and graduated *magna cum laude with highest honors*. He has been doing research since his freshman year in high school and has completed ten projects in the fields of tissue engineering, stem cell biology, spinal cord injury, behavioral science, health policy, neuroscience, nanotechnology, infectious disease and biotechnology. In addition to being inducted into the National Gallery for America's Young Inventors, Shiv won the American Academy of Neurology Neuroscience Research Prize, as well as awards at the International Science and Engineering Fair (second place in Medicine and Health three years in a row), Siemens Competition (regional finalist) and Junior Science and Humanities Symposium (national finalist). A participant in the Research Science Institute and member of the 2006 USA Today Academic First Team, Shiv has also published his research in *BMC Neuroscience* and the *Journal of Cell Transplantation*. In college Shiv remained active with research by founding the Harvard College Undergraduate Research Association, serving as chief executive officer of the international undergraduate research journal, the *Journal of Young Investigators,* and participating in the Harvard College Research Program as well as the Program for Research in Science and Engineering.

Maria Elena De Obaldia

Maria Elena (Ellen) De Obaldia is currently an Immunology Ph.D. candidate and a Howard Hughes Medical Institute (HHMI) Med into Grad Scholar at the University of Pennsylvania in Philadelphia, PA, where she conducts basic research on hematopoiesis or blood cell development. Ellen graduated in June 2008 from Harvard, where she concentrated in biology. While at Harvard, Ellen received grant support from the Harvard College Research Program (HCRP) and was a Program in Science and Engineering (PRISE) fellow. As a high school sophomore, Ellen was awarded first place and best of category awards in microbiology at the 2002 Intel ISEF in Louisville, Kentucky. As a junior, Ellen won second place award in microbiology at the 2003 Intel ISEF. Ellen also was selected as a regional finalist in the Siemens Competition as a senior in 2004. Ellen attended the Research Science Institute at MIT during the summer of 2003, and was named to the USA Today Academic First Team in May 2004. Ellen's research has been published in the *Journal of Virology* and *Circulation Research*.

Scott Duke Kominers

Scott Duke Kominers *(www.scottkom.com)* is a Ph.D. candidate in business economics at Harvard University. In 2009, he completed his A.B. at Harvard in mathematics, *summa cum laude* and Phi Beta Kappa, with a minor in ethnomumusicology. He then completed his A.M. in Business Economics, also at Harvard, in 2010. Scott has published 17 research articles (in mathematics, economics and musicology), as well as expository articles, puzzles and haiku. He was recently awarded the AMS-MAA-SIAM Frank and Brennie Morgan Prize for Outstanding Research in Mathematics by an Undergraduate Student and the Thomas Temple Hoopes Prize for his undergraduate thesis. He is an NSF Graduate Research Fellow, a Yahoo! Key Scientific Challenges Program Fellow, and a Terence M. Considine Fellow. Additionally, he has been supported by grants from the Harvard Real Estate Academic Initiative, the Harvard Mathematics Department, the Harvard Institute for Quantitative Social Science, the Harvard College Program for Research in Science and Engineering, and the Center for Excellence in Education.

Scott conducted number theory research at the 2004 Research Science Institute, for which he was named a semifinalist in the Siemens and Intel Science Talent Search competitions, a regional finalist in the Junior Sciences and Humanities Symposium, and a finalist in the Intel International Science and Engineering Fair (ISEF). At the ISEF, he was awarded the first place AMS Karl Menger Prize and the second place grand award in the mathematics category.

Dayan Li

Dayan (Jack) Li is a Molecular and Cellular Biology major in the Harvard Class of 2011. In high school, Jack spent two summers conducting angiogenesis research in Dr. David Roberts' Laboratory at the National Cancer Institute, National Institutes of Health. With this project, he was selected as a 2007 Intel Science Talent Search Semifinalist and was named an Intel Foundation Young Scientist for being one of three top project presenters at the 2007 Intel International Science and Engineering Fair. Since freshman year at Harvard, Jack has studied the Sonic Hedgehog signaling pathway in vertebrate development as a student researcher in the McMahon Laboratory at the Harvard Department of Stem Cell and Regenerative Biology. Outside the laboratory, Jack has served as Co-Chair of the Special Projects Committee and Chair of the Seminars Committee in the Harvard College Undergraduate Research Association. In addition, he has served as President of the Harvard Chapter of *The Triple Helix,* an international undergraduate journal of science in society. He is also the journal's 2010-2011 Executive Editor-in-Chief at the international division, and presented his *Triple Helix* work at the 2009 Annual Meeting of the American Association for the Advancement of Science. In 2010, Jack was awarded a Barry M. Goldwater Scholarship for his research in the McMahon Laboratory and for his academic work at Harvard.

Carol Y. Suh

Carol Yoon Joo Suh is a member of the Harvard Class of 2011. She is a molecular and cellular biology concentrator and is currently involved in stem cell research through the Harvard Stem Cell Institute. Carol has been involved with the Harvard College Undergraduate Research Association (HCURA) since her freshman year and served as president during her junior year. During college, she has received the Herchel Smith Research Fellowship, the Harvard College Research Program grants, and was a fellow in the Harvard College Program for Research in Science and Engineering (PRISE). In high school, Carol primarily focused on studying biomedical applications using microfluidics. And in her senior year of high school, Carol was selected as a 2007 Intel Science Talent Search Finalist and was also named to the USA Today Academic First Team in 2007. She was also an Intel International Science and Engineering Fair finalist from 2005 to 2007 and was awarded third place in medicine and health in 2006 and 2007.